THE EUROPEAN COMMUNITY AND EASTERN EUROPE

THE EUROPEAN COMMUNITY AND EASTERN EUROPE

John Pinder

PUBLISHED IN NORTH AMERICA FOR

THE ROYAL INSTITUTE OF INTERNATIONAL AFFAIRS

COUNCIL ON FOREIGN RELATIONS PRESS
• NEW YORK •

Chatham House Papers

A West European Programme Publication
Programme Director: Helen Wallace

The Royal Institute of International Affairs, at Chatham House in London, has provided an impartial forum for discussion and debate on current international issues for 70 years. Its resident research fellows, specialized information resources, and range of publications, conferences, and meetings span the fields of international politics, economics, and security. The Institute is independent of government.

Chatham House Papers are short monographs on current policy problems which have been commissioned by the RIIA. In preparing the papers, authors are advised by a study group of experts convened by the RIIA, and publication of a paper indicates that the Institute regards it as an authoritative contribution to the public debate. The Institute does not, however, hold opinions of its own; the views expressed in this publication are the responsibility of the author.

Library of Congress Cataloguing-in-Publication Data

Pinder, John.
    The European Community and Eastern Europe / by John Pinder
        p.   cm. — (Chatham House papers)
    Includes bibliographical references.
    ISBN 0-87609-112-5 : $14.95
    1. European Economic Community countries—Foreign economic relations—Europe, Eastern. 2. Europe, Eastern—Foreign economic relations—European Economic Community countries. I. Series.
HF1532.935.E8P56   1991
337.1'42—dc20
                                                                    91-21785
                                                                        CIP

91   92   93   94   95   96   97   PB   10   9   8   7   6   5   4   3   2   1

CONTENTS

ABBREVIATIONS

BERD	see EBRD
CMEA	Council of Mutual Economic Assistance (Bulgaria, Czecho-slovakia, GDR [until German unification], Hungary, Poland, Romania, the Soviet Union, together with Cuba, Mongolia, Vietnam)
CoCom	Coordinating Committee for Multilateral Export Controls
Comecon	see CMEA
Coreper	Committee of Permanent Representatives
CSCE	Conference on Security and Cooperation in Europe
EBRD	European Bank for Reconstruction and Development
EC	European Community
ECE	see UNECE
ecu	European currency unit (in April 1991, approximately $1.2, £0.7, DM 2.1)
EEA	European Economic Area
EEC	European Economic Community
Efta	European Free Trade Association
emu	economic and monetary union
EPC	European Political Cooperation
Gatt	General Agreement on Tariffs and Trade
GDR	German Democratic Republic
GDP	Gross Domestic Product
GSP	Generalized System of Preferences
G7	Group of 7
G24	Group of 24

IGC	Intergovernmental Conference
IMF	International Monetary Fund
mfn	most-favoured nation
Nato	North Atlantic Treaty Organization
OECD	Organization of Economic Cooperation and Development
OEEC	Organization for European Economic Cooperation
OJ	Official Journal of the European Communities
OPEC	Organization of Petroleum Exporting Countries
PHARE	Poland and Hungary: aid for economic reconstruction
SEA	Single European Act
TEMPUS	Transeuropean Mobility Programme for University Studies
UNECE	United Nations Economic Commission for Europe
US	United States of America
VRA	Voluntary Restraint Arrangement
WEU	Western European Union

NOTE ON GEOGRAPHICAL TERMINOLOGY

When the political map changes so fast, geographical terminology has a hard time keeping up. Any terminology for groups of countries may strike some as infelicitous or even offensive. But for the purpose of analysis, groups there have to be; and in this paper they are defined as follows:

Czechoslovakia (short for the Czech and Slovak Federal Republic), Hungary and Poland are called *Central Europe*. Austria, which is also part of Central Europe, is not included in the Central European group in this study; nor is any part of Yugoslavia.

Albania, Bulgaria, Romania and Yugoslavia are called *Balkan states,* or *the Balkans*. Greece, usually defined as a Balkan state, is not included; nor is the European part of Turkey.

These Central European and Balkan states are called *Eastern Europe*. The Soviet Union, despite its large territory in the eastern part of Europe, has yet larger territory in Asia and is not included in this term in the text (although the title of this paper does, for brevity, include the Soviet Union).

Eastern Europe and the Soviet Union together are called *the East, the eastern countries,* or *the eastern neighbours*.

PREFACE

This paper was first conceived when change in the relationship between the EC and its eastern neighbours was still slight and slow, and the aim could be no more than to indicate the potential if relations should improve. The radical changes since 1989 have made the task of writing it the more rewarding one of assessing remarkable progress and exploring the potential from this more promising base. The task has also become harder because change is so fast; and some of what is written may be outdated before it is read. This risk can be minimized with the help of those close enough to the events to provide the most up-to-date knowledge and evaluation. I am very grateful to the many people who have helped in this way, from Eastern Europe and the Soviet Union, from Brussels and Whitehall, from other EC countries and from the group that Chatham House assembled to consider the draft. I am particularly grateful to colleagues at Chatham House for their patience, helpfulness and encouragement to an author in travail. Responsibility for the views expressed is of course entirely mine.

The Institute acknowledges the financial support of Midland Bank plc, Samuel Montagu & Co Limited, the Gatsby Charitable Foundation and other sponsors of the West European Programme in the preparation and publication of this study.

April 1991   John Pinder

1

THE NEW EUROPE: EUROPEAN COMMUNITY, PLURALIST DEMOCRACY, MARKET ECONOMY

The European Community faces historic choices in its relations with its neighbours to the East.

A first great decision was taken for it by hundreds of thousands of Germans voting with their feet: leaving East Germany for the West. When the government of the Federal Republic concluded that only German unification could stop the rot, and Germany's partners accepted this view, East Germany inevitably became part of the European Community, joining the Federal Republic in October 1990. But the Community has to decide for itself on its relations with the countries of Eastern Europe and the Soviet Union in the light of their circumstances and of its own interests; and its decisions will help to shape the political map of Europe for many years to come.

The Community has offered association, or 'Europe Agreements', to Czechoslovakia, Hungary and Poland, on the grounds that they have made clear progress towards pluralist democracy and market economy, which are fundamental principles for the Community and hence for such a close relationship with it. The governments of the three countries have made it plain that they want not only association, but also eventually membership. The evolution of association and the prospects for membership will depend on the ways in which their polities and economies develop. There are good hopes that they will become stable pluralist democracies and competitive market economies so that their membership would not present the Community with many problems in a few years' time. But there are also fears of economic failure and, perhaps associated with it, of a reversion to authoritarian and nationalistic regimes.

1

Czechoslovakia, Hungary and Poland belong to Central Europe, as it is usually now defined. Of the former members of the Council of Mutual Economic Assistance (the CMEA, or Comecon) and the Warsaw Pact, these three have the best prospects for pluralist democracy and market economy. Yugoslavia, traditionally defined as a Balkan state, lies uneasily between the Central Europeans and its Balkan neighbours, Bulgaria, Romania and Albania. Although the Yugoslav League of Communists no longer provides the government of four of the Yugoslav republics, it still dominates Serbia, the largest; and there are dangerous conflicts between republics and nationalities. Despite long-standing use of market mechanisms, political obstacles have stood in the way of further economic reform. Bulgaria has taken steps towards political and economic reform, but is still far behind the Central Europeans. In Romania, multi-party elections have produced a government that is still dominated by people from the old communist party, even if there are new faces and, for the party, a new name; and the programme for reform to a market economy carries less conviction. Some first steps have been taken to change Albania's stalinist regime. In these countries, the prospect of pluralist democracy and competitive market economy seems more distant, and the danger of authoritarian nationalism greater, than in Central Europe.

Despite the great changes of the last five years, the same has to be said of the Soviet Union. Hopes for a pluralist polity and economy during this decade, or at least for an authoritarian government with a market economy, should not be abandoned. But almost anything seems possible. From a centralized union to separate republics; from pluralist democracy to authoritarian or even again to totalitarian government; from prosperity and peace to poverty and civil war: the Community will have to be prepared for all eventualities.

Since the Community is not merely an observer but can have some influence, it should develop a strategy towards Eastern Europe and the Soviet Union that corresponds to its interests.

Interests of the EC and its member states
It is in the interests of the Community that pluralist democracy and market economy should prevail throughout Europe.

The potential for trade with market economies to the East is indicated by one fact: the Community's trade with Sweden alone is of the same order of magnitude as it has been with the state-trading countries of

2

Comecon as a whole. Market economies, based on the production of goods and services that people want to buy, are much better adapted to international trade. The potential for trade with these new market economies over the next few years has been explored by the Centre for Economic Policy Research.[1] If the Community's economy is to remain dynamic through the 1990s, it will need a new impulse following the single market programme; and this potential could help to provide it. In so far as association brings economic integration, the potential will be enhanced, as the Cecchini report on the completion of the single market has demonstrated.[2]

Nor should the down side of economic failure to the East be forgotten. If these countries do not develop competitive market economies, they are likely to be beset by poverty, which keeps them as poor markets and induces large numbers of their people to want to emigrate to the West; and they will be more susceptible to authoritarianism and nationalism, less likely to stay with pluralist democracy.

The relaxation of Soviet power in Eastern Europe and in the Soviet Union itself has shown how the system, in repressing nationalism, failed to temper its violence. Where pluralist democracy is established, it can better accommodate different nationalities in a peaceful order. National conflict within some of the eastern countries is a serious threat to stability and, eventually, to peace, which could also threaten the security of Western Europe; and there is a danger of conflict between independent states, which is less likely to take violent form among pluralist democracies. In so far as the Community can help to strengthen democracy in its eastern neighbours, it will be enhancing its own security.

There is a further link between democracy and the market economy. Although a market economy can function under an authoritarian government, there are tensions between a free economy and a servile polity. Where these tensions are resolved in favour of political freedom, the market economy will be more secure – and the Community's economic interests better satisfied.

Competitive market economies and stable pluralist democracies among its eastern neighbours will, then, be helpful to the interests, both economic and security, of the Community. They will also have the great merit of expressing the political values that are at the root of the Community and its member states. The Hague Congress of Europe, which under Winston Churchill's presidency launched the process of European unification in 1948, resolved that 'the resultant Union or Federation should be open to all European nations democratically governed and which undertake to respect a Charter of Human Rights'.[3] It would not be good for the Community to neglect its interest in the establishment of rights and freedoms throughout Europe.

These interests, of economics, security and values, are shared by the Community as a whole. But there are differences of intensity and of emphasis among the different member states.

Geography and history have given Germany the greatest stake in relations with the East. Trade statistics bear stark witness to its economic interest. Before the depression of the 1930s, 17% of German exports went to the area comprising Eastern Europe and the Soviet Union. In 1989, it was no more than 4%; and the Federal Republic's exports to Denmark exceeded those to Czechoslovakia, Hungary and Poland combined.[4] The scope for expansion of Germany's trade with its eastern neighbours is enormous; and there will be great pressure to migrate to Germany if their economies fail. Germany is likewise more exposed than other Community members to the risks of political instability and eventual conflicts to the East. Counterbalancing this intense German interest in relations with the eastern neighbours has been the policy of the Federal Republic to remain anchored in the western system, where Western Germany has experienced such prosperity and stability since World War Two. In addition to membership of Nato, this has involved commitment to the European Community, currently expressed in the German government's policy of strengthening the Community through the Intergovernmental Conferences on economic and monetary union and on political union.

Although many Germans have their doubts about the merits of replacing the deutschmark by a European currency, the German government has accepted the aims of a single currency and a European central bank, firmly linked with progress towards political union, including a common foreign and security policy, and strengthening the EC institutions and the European Parliament in particular.[5] There are economic motives for this Westpolitik. The Community economy is important for German prosperity; and the cost of an effective policy towards the eastern neighbours as Germans see it is too great to be borne by Germany alone, but needs to be shared among the members of the Community, as well as by the United States and Japan.[6] But the basic motive is political: a politically united Community is seen as the soundest context for Germany, including for the development of its relations with the East. The commitment to political union cannot be taken as unconditional, however. As a former State Secretary of the Federal Republic's foreign ministry has recently written, Germany could, if progress towards the 'deepening of integration' is impeded, resign itself to the maxim, 'as old as it is pernicious', that 'the strong is strongest alone'.[7] Avoidance of this possibility was a motive for combining the welcome for East Germany in the Community with the convening of the Intergovernmental Conference on political union at the meetings of the European Council in Dublin in the first half of 1990.[8]

Nor can the French commitment to solidarity with Germany within the Community as the wisest reaction to events in the East be taken entirely for granted. There is an older French tradition, of alliances in the East to counter German strength, which seemed to be reflected in President Mitterrand's journeys to East Germany and to Kiev while the question of German unification still hung in the balance. But four decades of successful Franco-German partnership proved stronger; and France has continued to pursue its policy of promoting economic and monetary union, which, in addition to some economic motives, is seen by the French as a firm anchor for Germany in the Community system, and a safer way to contain German power than alliances further East. But it has not passed unnoticed in Germany that France is reticent about steps towards a political union to which Germany is attached, such as powers for the European Parliament, or that, while the French expect the Germans to give up monetary sovereignty, they still want to keep their own military sovereignty intact.[9] These differences could lead to tensions that would prevent the Intergovernmental Conferences from yielding results positive enough to prevent the Germans from leaning towards the policy of 'strongest alone', thus loosening the bonds of collaboration in Community policy towards the East.

Italy and the Benelux countries favour both economic and monetary union and political union, and hence outcomes of the Intergovernmental Conferences most likely to keep France and Germany together in working for common policies towards the East. Spain and the Irish Republic have by and large gone along with Italy and Benelux in this; and they have been joined during the past year both by Denmark, which has drawn the conclusion from German unification that Germany should be ensconced within a strong Community, and by Greece. While none of these countries has the same intense interest as Germany in relations with the East, Italy in particular has made ambitious proposals for Community policy, in the form of a fund amounting to one-quarter of 1% of Community GDP for aid to the eastern neighbours.[10] The Dutch government has suggested that policy towards Eastern Europe should be among the first fields in which a common Community foreign policy should be decided by majority vote, on the grounds that there is already much convergence among the policies of member states and that external economic policy, already subject to majority voting, is such an important element in foreign policy towards the East.[11]

Whereas during the past four decades France has sought to integrate Germany into the Community, and has during much of that time seen the sharing of sovereignty – other than in the military field – as the price to be paid for this, Britain has usually sought to minimize the merging of sovereignty in the Community. While the opening to the East led the French to strengthen their support for monetary integration, Mrs Margaret Thatcher's reaction, as Prime Minister, was that the Community should shelve proposals for economic and monetary union or for political union, since these could make it harder for eastern countries to join. Even if her departure brings changes of substance as well as style, Britain will, unless there is a definite change of strategy, remain cool towards the monetary integration wanted by the French and towards important elements in the political union wanted by the Germans; and this can hardly conduce to the development of a solid common policy towards the East that would commit the Germans and the French as well as other member states over the longer term. On the other side, the British government, eager to support the replacement of communist by democratic regimes with market economies, took the initiative in preparing the offer of association agreements. Mrs Thatcher's speeches at Aspen and in Prague gave a positive thrust to Community policy towards the East;[12] and Britain is among the strongest advocates of an open trading policy towards the eastern countries, against the more protectionist inclinations of some other member states, demonstrated for example by Greece, Portugal and Spain in the negotiations for Europe Agreements.

The link between the further integration, or deepening, of the Community and the opening to the East complicates the development of the Community's eastern policy. But, given the central position of Germany in both respects, the link cannot be broken. It is part of the context in which the Community's policy has to be made.

Questions for Community policy

The aim of this paper is to consider answers to some questions about Community policy towards Eastern Europe and the Soviet Union. What, for example, can the Community do to help them towards stable pluralist democracy and competitive market economy? How can it judge whether their progress justifies shifting the relationship from one stage to another: from trade and cooperation agreements, through association, to eventual membership? What would be the content of the trade relationship at the different stages? What kind of aid, how big, how much from the Community and how much from the member states? How can the Community best relate to its western partners in this? What if the Soviet Union, Yugoslavia or other eastern countries shed some republics or disintegrate? What if the Soviet Union and perhaps other states revert to a hostile attitude to the Community or the West? What are the implications of various answers to such questions for the Community's policies, instruments, powers and institutions? And what are the implications for British policy?

The answers to such questions about what to do in the future have to be sought in what seems relevant in the circumstances of the present and the experience of the past. Chapter 2 summarizes the history of relations between the Community and the Comecon group up to 1985. While this helps to explain subsequent events, readers in a hurry may wish to pass to Chapter 3, which takes the story from the beginnings of radical change in the mid-1980s up to the end of 1990, when negotiations for Europe Agreements were about to begin. Chapter 4 looks at the process of political and economic reform from one-party monopoly to pluralist systems. Chapter 5 considers the Europe Agreements with Central Europeans; Chapter 6, relations with the Soviet Union and the Balkan states; and Chapter 7, the Community's aid to the East. Chapter 8 offers some conclusions.

2
THE COMMUNITY AND COMECON TO 1985: STUBBORN DIPLOMACY

When the Community was founded in the late 1950s, the Soviet Union saw it as a reinforcement of the capitalist camp, detrimental to Soviet interests. The first detailed exposition of that view, published in 1957, depicted the Community as a closed group serving the monopolist class interests of the exploiters, and as an economic arm of Nato with an aggressive posture towards Eastern Europe. 'West German imperialism' would use the Community to strengthen its war potential and would seek to arm itself with atomic weapons. Marxist analysis concluded that the Community's internal contradictions would cause it to disintegrate.[1] But, far from disintegrating, the Community was remarkably successful. By 1962, the Soviet view had been revised significantly. While still emphasizing capitalist contradictions and complaining that the Community would damage the trade of the 'socialist countries', the Soviet observers now saw it as an economic and political reality that had made much progress in implementing the EEC Treaty. Following advice from the Italian Communists, they went so far as to accept that the common market promoted investment, modernization and external trade, as well as wage increases.[2] Yet the Soviet Union, having decided not to accord the Community juridical recognition, continued to treat it for over two more decades with varying degrees of coldness: one aspect of the 'era of stagnation' under Brezhnev, lasting from 1964 to 1984. With some exceptions, the East European countries complied with this policy.

The 1960s: EC member states' initiatives

The Community, for its part, paid only marginal attention to Eastern Europe and the Soviet Union through the 1960s. The EEC Treaty had made no special provision for relations with these states apart from the 'Protocol on German internal trade and connected problems', which exempted the GDR's trade with the Federal Republic from the provisions of the EC's common commercial policy, thus exonerating the Federal Republic from imposing Community tariffs and levies on its imports from East Germany. The Community's common external tariff was applied to imports from the eastern countries, as from other sources, and they were also accorded the cuts in tariffs resulting from international trade negotiations. The same regime applied to agricultural imports from the East as to those from other sources. Imports of steel were restricted by the Community during a crisis of over-supply, but the numerous quotas on other imports remained throughout this period in the hands of the member states.[3]

As detente began to replace the cold war, EC members were among the West European states that sought to outdo each other both economically and politically in their relations with the East. At first the British set the pace, with a fifteen-year credit for the Soviet Union in 1964. France followed with an agreement with the Soviet Union for scientific and technological exchanges in 1965, and in 1966 scrapped many of its quotas on imports from Eastern Europe. Italy signed a similar agreement with the Soviet Union in 1966. But the most important of this series of agreements was the Moscow Treaty between the Soviet Union and the Federal Republic of Germany, signed in 1970. This was the first fruit of Chancellor Willy Brandt's Ostpolitik, which led to more normal relations between the Federal Republic and Eastern Europe; and it was followed in 1973 by a ten-year agreement on economic, industrial and technological cooperation between the Federal Republic and the Soviet Union, which included such major projects as the integrated steelworks based on the iron ore at Kursk and the first long-term agreement for the German purchase of Soviet natural gas.

Significantly for the Community, Brandt's Ostpolitik was accompanied by a Westpolitik, designed to anchor the Federal Republic securely among its western partners. This included a set of proposals to strengthen the Community, with projects for economic and monetary union and for foreign policy cooperation, as well as to widen it through the admission of Britain and other applicants. Britain, Denmark and the Irish Republic were indeed admitted, and the mechanism for foreign policy cooperation

9

was put in place under the name of European Political Cooperation (EPC). But the proposal for economic and monetary union (emu) was shelved because of policy differences and international monetary turbulence. Germany's relationship with the East has again been among the motives for reviving the emu proposal and hence for the Intergovernmental Conference on the subject that opened in 1990, as also for the parallel conference on deepening the Community through measures of political union; and the possible widening of the Community, through accession of East European countries, has again been seen as an argument for deepening it.

Until the mid-1970s, in the period dominated by General de Gaulle and the immediate aftermath, the member governments did not allow the Community as such to take any important initiatives towards Eastern Europe. The Commission was reduced, for the most part, to ensuring that the member states' agreements did not contravene the treaties and to proposing consultation among the member governments; and it was agreed in 1962 that the span of export credits would not exceed five years. In 1966, however, when de Gaulle's reductionist policy towards the Community was in full flood, the French Foreign Minister, Maurice Couve de Murville, announced that export credits were an element of foreign policy and that foreign policy was the prerogative of the member states, so that France could not be bound by such restrictions. It was not until 1975, after the end of the transitional period and when the common commercial policy had entered fully into force, that the Commission was able to secure a judgment from the Court of Justice to the effect that export credit policy was a Community competence, since the EEC Treaty stipulated that the common commercial policy was to be 'based on uniform principles' in regard to a number of matters, including 'export policy' (art. 113 EEC).

Even during the 1960s, the Commission managed to make a few minor agreements with East European authorities, despite their refusal to recognize the Community and the gaullist policy of restricting the Commission's competences. Thus, by the mid-1960s, East European representatives began to establish informal contacts with the Commission in order to deal with problems encountered by their agricultural exports, which resulted in modest agreements to ease their access. The Poles in 1965 were the first to reach such an agreement, followed by the Bulgarians, Hungarians and Romanians.

More importantly, the Community concluded a trade agreement with Yugoslavia in 1970, confirming the most-favoured-nation treatment that had hitherto been conceded unilaterally, and providing a significant concession on imports of 'baby beef', as well as setting up a joint committee of Community and Yugoslav representatives to consider problems that might arise. The Community was making a political point. Yugoslavia, not being a member of the Soviet bloc or of Comecon, had no inhibitions about recognizing the Community, which wished to make it clear that those who refused to recognize it were excluded from certain benefits – even if the benefits for Yugoslavia from this initial agreement were not very great.

In a period when member states were liberalizing their imports from Eastern Europe, the Commission was also able to secure from the Council a commitment not to impose any new quotas on imports of products on the 'liberalization list', comprising those that were already quota-free in all the member states. With this small step, the Commission was preparing for what it intended should be a liberal stance when the common commercial policy came into full effect after the end of the transitional period.

The 1970s: slow talks between the EC and Comecon

The Community decided – concurrently with the entry of Britain, Denmark and Ireland in 1973 – that the bilateral trade agreements between member states and East European countries, which were all due to expire by 1975 at the latest, would not be renewed, thus leaving the way open for trade agreements between the Community as such and the East Europeans. Towards the end of 1974, the Commission sent a letter to each state-trading country proposing negotiations on a list of subjects including import quotas, agricultural imports, most-favoured-nation treatment, safeguard mechanisms, and problems of payment and trade finance.[4] Consonant with the Soviet policy of not recognizing the Community, the Commission received no replies from the member states of Comecon.

This silence did not signify a blank refusal to talk to the Community, but rather a Soviet desire that the most important part of the talking should be done by Comecon, not by its member states; and this reflected a new Soviet interest in building up Comecon, following the crushing of the Prague Spring in 1968, and a search for ways of limiting the independence of the East Europeans without recourse to further military intervention. Comecon had previously had very little substance. Stalin founded it in 1949 in reaction to the creation of the Organization for

European Economic Cooperation (OEEC) in Western Europe in 1948, but that hardly affected the bilateral relations between the Soviet Union and its East European partners.[5] In 1962, on observing the early success of the EEC, Nikita Khrushchev launched a proposal to make Comecon a supranational planning organ for the group; but this was resisted vehemently by Romania on grounds of national sovereignty, and covertly by the Hungarians and Poles, and therefore came to naught. Then came Leonid Brezhnev's pressure for economic integration as an instrument for securing political stability within the bloc.

Negotiations among the Comecon members started in 1969 and concluded in 1971 with agreement on what was called the Comprehensive Programme.[6] This provided in much detail for cooperation in economic planning, planning of the member states' mutual trade, specialization agreements, joint ventures and a range of other activities. The Hungarians ensured that there was also reference to market mechanisms and convertibility; but little came of that and the emphasis remained heavily on the coordination of central planning and of the corresponding policy instruments.

Although Brezhnev's motive was doubtless primarily political, and repressive, there were two other elements in Soviet thinking about economic integration at that time which were more promising for the future. One was the need to look more effectively beyond the constraints of a system that had been designed to build socialism in one country, and to make a reality of the principle of the international division of labour. While this need was naturally felt much more keenly in the smaller East European countries, the desire for stronger international links was also growing in the Soviet Union.

The second element of interesting Soviet thinking was a new and more constructive evaluation of integration in the European Community. The main source of this thinking was within the Institute of World Economy and International Relations.[7] 'Capitalist integration' was now seen as an 'objective phenomenon', rooted in the nature of technological and economic development. The private sector (or, in their terminology, private monopoly capitalism) needed the wider market in which to pursue that development: hence the need to remove the barriers to trade among the Community's member states. At the same time, the Community had to take account of the range of economic policies that the capitalist states had introduced as a framework for the activities of the private sector (this they called state monopoly capitalism); and this led to the Community's need for a range of common policies. The Community, the Soviet analysts then concluded, would be prevented by the contradictions among its capitalist member states from making such common policies effective enough. The contradiction between an international EC economy and the member states' national polities would thus remain. But the message was clear enough. The Community was an attempt, and a fairly useful one, by capitalist countries to come to terms with the growing need for an international economy.

This new thinking about the Community – seeing its integration as part of a 'world tendency' – fitted well with the growing interest in integration among Comecon countries, which in turn suited Brezhnev's political aims. The Community's offer of negotiations could also, it appeared, be turned to account in this respect. Brezhnev had already suggested in 1972 that relations could be established if the Community were to 'recognize the realities in Eastern Europe, especially the interests of CMEA countries';[8] and in August 1973, during the Danish presidency of the Community, the secretary general of Comecon had visited Copenhagen to discuss possible negotiations. Evidently, Comecon wanted to downgrade the EC Commission by ignoring its competence with respect to trade agreements and by relating to the member governments instead. Soviet policy was at the same time intent on strengthening Comecon by giving it new responsibilities for trade negotiations at the expense of its member states.

The Community had a fundamental political objection to trade negotiations with Comecon. The Soviet Union's East European partners had hitherto enjoyed a fair degree of autonomy in their external trade policies; and the transfer of some competence in this field to Comecon, which was inevitably dominated by the preponderant weight of the Soviet Union, would reduce this autonomy and reinforce Soviet hegemony – an outcome the Community wanted to avoid. The Commission, for its part, was also determined to avoid the reduction of its competences that the approach adopted by Comecon appeared to imply. The Commission argued, moreover, that because Comecon lacked formal competence for trade policy, trade negotiations with it would be inappropriate; the agreements would, at the end of the day, have to be concluded with the Comecon member states, with which the competence in fact lay.[9]

Not surprisingly, therefore, the Community refused to negotiate with Comecon about trade. Instead, it proposed to negotiate about statistics, forecasts, standards and the environment. Talks continued at a slow pace, without either side giving enough to make agreement possible, until in

1979, five years after the Commission had addressed its original letter to the Comecon governments, and when the talks had anyway reached an impasse, the Soviet intervention in Afghanistan changed the political climate in a way that was to preclude further such discussions for another five years and more.

Soviet and EC interests and the structure of East-West trade

The political reasons for the failure of the Community and Comecon to reach agreement in the 1970s are clear enough. But it must still be asked why economic interests were not enough to overcome the political obstacles. The short answer is that, as things stood then, neither of the two major parties saw much economic interest in the negotiations.

The Soviet exports to the EC have been within the range of 1–2% of Soviet GDP, depending on the price of oil and on the way in which the GDP is measured; and Soviet imports from the EC have fallen within a similar range. This is not a great weight in the Soviet economy; but neither is it by any means to be ignored, particularly in view of the qualitative significance of the imports, embodying effective technologies, filling supply gaps that could disrupt production, and helping to feed the people. The reason why the Soviet Union had scant motive for trade negotiations was not that the trade with the EC was unimportant, but that it was little affected by the Community's commercial policy. The bulk of Soviet exports to the Community – up to nine-tenths in value when energy prices were high – comprised oil, gas and other primary products, to which the Community applies no tariff, levy or import restriction. The small proportion made up by manufactures does encounter tariffs; but most of these manufactures have not been of the labour-intensive types on which the Community imposes its higher tariffs. With the structure of Soviet exports as it has been until now, therefore, the Soviet Union has had no pressing motive to seek concessions in the Community's commercial policy.

The Community's trade with Comecon as a whole comprised a somewhat similar percentage of its GDP: significant, but, it may bear repeating, of the same order of magnitude as the Community's trade with Sweden, which has no more than 2% of Comecon's population, but whose economic system is far more conducive to prosperity and to trade. The Soviet-style command economy was resistant to the development of external trade that has been normal elsewhere, and was an increasingly poor performer in international markets in which new technologies were becoming more and more important.

It should not be surprising that a system originally designed for self-sufficiency in one country should be ill-adapted to international trade, or that producers whose eyes are focused on the instructions of the planners should fail to cater for the requirements of the consumers. Where the consumers have the choice that is available in sophisticated international markets, the weakness of exports from the command economies is a foregone conclusion. Behind this weakness lies a more general failure of the command economies, with their rigid form of organization and their resistance to innovation, to move ahead with the application of the new technologies, thus stunting their capacity to compete.

It was already becoming clear in the 1970s, when the talks between the Community and Comecon were hanging fire, that, apart from the boost to Soviet imports resulting from high earnings from energy sales, and to imports of those other East European countries that borrowed heavily at the time, the Comecon market could not be regarded as a dynamic one. On top of this, the Community, like other market economies, found it difficult to identify clear economic objectives for trade negotiations with the command economies: the same problem that the Soviet Union had in relation to the Community, although for quite different reasons. The purpose of trade negotiations among market economies is to reduce the protection of the trading partners in such a way as to influence the patterns of their imports as favourably as possible. This is done by seeking reductions of particular tariffs or liberalization of particular quotas – and now increasingly of other non-tariff distortions. In the case of the command economies, the pattern of imports was determined by a foreign trade plan as part of the general plan for the economy. To seek a change in the pattern would be to seek a change in the plan. It is true that the trade negotiations within Comecon did attempt to adjust the trade plans of the member states in order to meet the requirements of other member states – although they were often not very successful in doing so. But the command economies did not appear willing to negotiate with the market economies about their own plans. Nor, it must be said, would the market economies have been eager to be drawn into that game, which they regarded as an inadequate way to manage the trade of a modern economy. Since, therefore, objectives that were normal in trade negotiations among market economies did not seem to be feasible, the Community lacked a major economic motive for negotiating with Comecon or its members.

The Community did develop objectives, such as better access for its exporters to their customers or more industrial and statistical information, in countries in which, as in the Soviet Union in particular, the existing practice was highly restrictive. But such aims could also be pursued in other contexts, such as the Conference on Security and Cooperation in Europe (CSCE). Tariff negotiations took place in the Gatt, with the Hungarians, Poles and Romanians participating, and the other Comecon countries also getting the benefit of the agreed reductions. The Romanians, together with the Yugoslavs, also got the unilateral advantage of the Community's Generalized System of Preferences (GSP). Although the Soviet Union had banned general trade agreements, its East European partners managed to negotiate with the Community about trade in particular sectors – agriculture, steel and textiles – in which problems of Community protection arose; and in 1980 Romania concluded an agreement on trade in industrial products that were not covered by the sectoral agreements, which provided a context for the relaxation of EC quotas, and was accompanied by a second agreement to set up a joint committee to oversee the development of trade.

Beyond the concept of the trade agreement, there were also the cooperation agreements concluded between the member states of the Community and of Comecon. In so far as the aim of the western partners in their trade negotiations with command economies was to maintain contacts and to keep their countries' enterprises on the 'planners' map', the negotiations for cooperation agreements served the purpose as well or better; for one of their main aims was to arrange for ongoing relationships between the western enterprises and those who were responsible for trade in the East. The main substance of cooperation agreements at the time was the granting of credits by the western governments to the Comecon countries; and the EC's member governments ensured that, providing they observed the Community's guidelines on the terms of export credits, this remained a matter for them rather than for the Community. In short, the member governments were quite satisfied with the cooperation agreements, which they sometimes stretched to the point of incursions into trade policy; and the Commission, given the existence of the various fora for negotiating and the difficulty of finding any compelling economic objectives for trade negotiations, had little economic incentive to outweigh the political objections to accepting a trade relationship with Comecon on the terms that were on offer in the 1970s.

The East European countries and their desire to negotiate

The situation of the Soviet Union's European partners in Comecon was completely different. Their imports from Western Europe, and from the EC in particular, are a major component in their economies. Quantitatively, these imports have comprised over one-tenth of Hungary's GDP and, for most of the East Europeans, the proportion has been in the range of 5–10%. Qualitatively, this trade is, for reasons similar to those already given for the Soviet Union, yet more significant. If they fail to earn or borrow the hard currencies to pay for the imports, their prospects for economic development are blighted. In the 1970s, most of them covered their payments gaps by borrowing. But they realized that they needed to raise their export earnings; so access to the Community's market was vital to them.

Unlike those of the Soviet Union, these countries' exports encountered the Community's toughest protection. While about a quarter of their exports to the Community were materials, a further quarter were foodstuffs and the remaining half were manufactures, largely of the kinds against which the Community directed its most protective tariffs and quotas: products such as textiles, footwear, chinaware and steel. These, like agriculture, happened to be the sectors in which the Community's producers were the hardest pressed and were therefore given the tightest protection. Apart from Romania and Yugoslavia, both beneficiaries of the GSP, and East Germany with the free entry for its exports to the Federal Republic, the East Europeans were also at a disadvantage in relation to the developing countries, many of whose manufactures entered the Community tariff-free under the GSP, and a number of whose economies were more dynamic than those of the East Europeans. So East Europeans, unlike the Soviet Union, had an urgent need to improve the access of their exports to the Community; and, unlike the Community, they had very clear objectives for their negotiations, in the form of the liberalization of quotas and the reduction of tariffs and levies.

Thus the East Europeans were keen to negotiate with the Community. It may well be asked why such negotiations should bring significant results, since negotiations are fruitful usually because both parties have objectives that are compatible and can thus be achieved together, whereas the Community lacked any convincing economic objectives. Part of the answer is that the Community seldom sits down at the negoti-ating table without eventually conceding something; and, in this case, it had a political objective in terms of recognition and of the counter-balancing of Soviet power,

17

which, as its agreements with Yugoslavia had shown, led it to make trade concessions.[10]

Although in its initial trade agreement with Yugoslavia, signed in 1970, the Community provided only modest benefits, in 1971 it was granted the GSP, which was far more important; and Romania's independence from Soviet policy likewise led the Community in 1974 to grant it the GSP on a limited number of products. In 1973, as much as one-third of all the imports entering the EC with zero or reduced tariffs under the scheme came from Yugoslavia; and both Yugoslavia and Romania were among the principal beneficiaries during that decade. The results of trade negotiations were less dramatic, but none the less significant. In 1973, a second trade agreement with Yugoslavia provided some more reductions in tariffs and import levies. When this was replaced by a cooperation agreement in 1980 there were some further concessions on agricultural products, while the proportion of imports of manufactures that were to enter the Community tariff-free rose to some 70%; and in 1982 a protocol entailed some loosening of its protection against Yugoslav textiles, about half of which were to enter free of duty. The agreement of 1980 was called a cooperation agreement because its scope had been broadened to include finance, labour, science and technology. The finance comprised loans from the European Investment Bank for improving transport infrastructure – of interest to the Community in order to link Greece with other member states. Labour was significant because many Yugoslav migrant workers in the Community had lost their jobs or encountered other problems during the recession of the 1970s. Science and technology are normally on the list of subjects for discussion under cooperation agreements, often without much concrete result.

The lack of formal reciprocity in all these agreements did not pass unnoticed. A Yugoslav authority was to claim that their trade deficit with the Community was their principal form of reciprocity.[11] While this is in itself an unconvincing argument, the Community has in fact conceded quite a lot to the Yugoslavs: partly, no doubt, in line with its policy of concessions to the Mediterranean countries, but also in response to Yugoslavia's autonomy in relation to the Soviet Union and to its efforts to introduce market mechanisms into its economy.

For as long as the other East Europeans had not made the breakthrough on the road to market economy and pluralist democracy, the Community was not going to make concessions of much substance to them. After the breakthrough, the Community's policy was to change completely. But meanwhile, in the 1970s East Europeans were eager to secure any concessions that they might be able to get by negotiating with the Community. Negotiations were important to them. Yet the EC and the Soviet Union did not share their economic interest in the matter; so the smaller countries remained the victims of a political difference between their big partners.

This impasse, increasingly frustrating for East Europeans with stagnant economies and, in most cases, heavy burdens of debt, was to be prolonged by an aggravation of the political divergence, in the form of the Soviet intervention in Afghanistan, followed by the declaration of martial law in Poland in 1981.

1979–84: sanctions, CoCom and the pipeline

In reaction to the Afghanistan intervention and the martial law in Poland, the United States applied sanctions against the Soviet Union in the form of export controls; and, by the end of 1981, the US was pressing the European Community hard to follow suit. The EC member states were sceptical about the efficacy of export controls, and in particular about the effectiveness with which they could be applied by all the member states. But there was little doubting the Community's capacity to stem the flow of imports, as its history of protection for sensitive sectors had demonstrated. Since the Soviet Union's ability to import from the West is determined by its holdings of hard currencies, a reduction in its imports from the Soviet Union would, the Community argued, reduce the Soviet capacity to import and would thus squeeze the Soviet economy.

One difference between that method and the export controls applied by the Americans was that the Soviet Union could choose which of its imports to cut, thus dispensing with those most marginal to its needs, whereas the export controls could aim at the products judged most sensitive for the Soviet economy. Another difference was that the Soviet Union could, unless the Community's import cuts were to be large, keep to its import plan by raising its borrowing or its sales of gold. But the Community's import cuts, at around $100 million, were not large in relation to its total imports from the Soviet Union. Apart from the difficulty of getting the member governments to agree on the list of restrictions to be applied, the range of products to which the method was applicable was limited to the manufactures that comprised a small proportion of the trade, because an attempt to cut the imports of energy and materials would merely have led to a switch between Soviet and other suppliers in the world market. Lord Carrington, then president of the

Council of Foreign Ministers during the British turn in the Community's presidency, said that the cuts were a warning to the Soviet Union: if unacceptable behaviour continued, the cuts would be more severe.[12] Yet it was doubtful if the cuts could have been much more severe while still remaining effective. These sanctions were in large part a gesture; and as such they were significant, but no more. If the Soviet Union should ever return to the sort of behaviour that evoked them, the Community will have to consider more effective instruments of retaliation.

The CoCom controls, applied by Nato members (less Iceland, but including all the eleven EC members of Nato, together with Australia and Japan) to prevent the transfer of technologies useful for military purposes to member states of the Warsaw pact, were at the same time tightened up. This raised an increasingly difficult issue in the form of the 'dual-purpose' technologies that are used mainly for civilian purposes but can also have military applications. The very important microelectronic technologies were in this category, thus inducing conflicts between the guardians of security and some of those promoting such technological developments, and between the American authorities, who took a severe view of the security requirements, and the Europeans, who generally set more store on East-West trade as tending to both economic benefit and political stability.

These differences were contained through agreements made in CoCom. But the conflict between Americans and Europeans over the gas pipeline project in the early 1980s was less easily controlled. European companies were contracted to help in building the pipeline, which was to bring up to $10 billion worth of gas annually from the Soviet Union to Western Europe. One element in the contracts comprised jet engines to drive the gas down the pipelines at greater speed, thus raising their throughput; and these engines were to contain an element of American technology. The US government held that the Europeans would become too dependent on the Soviet gas and thus subject to Soviet pressure; and some in the US administration felt that the hard currency earned would strengthen the Soviet economy in ways that would enhance its military capacity and its ability to damage the West. The Americans therefore acted to prevent the use of their technology in this project. The result was a sharp quarrel between the Americans and their European allies. The Europeans, seeing no sufficient cause to break their contracts, confident that the Soviet Union would be at least as dependent on them as vice versa, and believing in the political and economic benefits of the trade, made it clear that they would not be deterred from going ahead. The

Americans eventually accepted the finding of an OECD report, that the degree of West European dependency on Soviet gas would not expose their allies to undue pressure, and the quarrel died down. The lesson seemed clear, on both sides of the Atlantic, that better ways must be found of resolving differences of approach to the strategic and political implications of East–West trade.

EC policies in the mid-1980s

By the mid-1980s, the EC's relationship with the Comecon countries appeared to have stabilized at a modest level of activity.[13] Much of EC policy was applied unilaterally rather than by agreement, given that the Comecon policy had resisted trade agreements between the Community and the Comecon member states. The Community continued to impose its import quotas specifically directed at state-trading countries. The regime for the coming year was established by a decision of the Council in December, although the Commission used to amend it during the course of the year (43 times in 1984, 63 times in 1985), often after consultation with the East European Countries Consultative Committee of officials from member states. Almost all these decisions involved relaxations of the quotas. The quotas were, indeed, a relic of the period when the member states used to protect their industries in this way. For preventing injury to its industries, the Community had its legislation against dumped or subsidized exports from the state-trading countries, which was revised in 1984 to make it simpler and more effective.[14] Anti-dumping cases were brought against these countries at a rate of about one a month, and were usually resolved by the exporters agreeing to raise their prices. In some cases, however, anti-dumping duties were applied – for example, hardboard from the Soviet Union and some iron and steel products from the GDR in 1984, and copper sulphate from Poland in 1985. Other duties expired or were amended or repealed: electric motors from the Soviet Union in 1984, upright pianos from the same source in 1985.

The Community applied its most-favoured-nation tariff rates to imports from the state-trading countries, as well as its normal levies on imports of agricultural products. But there were also the arrangements to limit the levies on a number of agricultural products from Comecon countries, such as had been pioneered by the Poles in 1965; and to these were added agreements negotiated with Comecon countries on the import of goat and sheep meat. The most important sectoral agreements

21

negotiated between the Community and Comecon countries related, however, to steel and textiles. There were annual negotiations with Bulgaria, Czechoslovakia, Hungary, Poland and Romania to set the levels of 'voluntary' restrictions on their exports of iron and steel products to the Community, in line with the Community's general policy of restricting such imports as part of its effort to deal with the over-capacity in its steel sector from the late 1970s through the 1980s. There were also negotiations with the same five countries in 1982 to set the quotas for the import of textiles into the Community, as part of the Multi-Fibre Arrangement (MFA) under the Gatt. These agreements ran until the end of 1986, by which time new agreements had been negotiated to last the next five years.

Romania was the only Comecon country to have a general industrial trade agreement with the Community, and the joint committee, which like the trade agreement had been negotiated in 1980, had annual meetings. The Community normally announced quota relaxations at these meetings: in December 1985 it was able to declare that some two hundred quotas would be abolished at the end of the year. The Community delegates also took the opportunity to make complaints: in 1986 these included the difficulty that embassies and enterprises from the member states found in employing local staff in Bucharest. The Romanians for their part would confirm their undertaking, given when they joined the Gatt, to increase imports from the Community no less fast than from other Gatt countries, and would agree to improve their provision of economic information: in short, they had little to offer. In 1985, their foreign minister told the EC Commissioner responsible for external relations that Romania wanted to replace the trade agreement by a trade and cooperation agreement, following the Yugoslav example.

The Community's policy and official relations with the Comecon countries were, then, inching forward in the mid-1980s. Discussions had started in 1983 with Czechoslovakia and Hungary about extending the scope of the agreements with them, which were still stuck at the stage of sectoral agreements for steel, textiles and some agricultural products. The Community had decided, since 1983, to provide food aid and medical supplies to Polish people through non-governmental organizations and the church; and the tension that had followed the martial law there was beginning to relax. But in none of this was there any sign of the qualitative leap that would follow the change of Soviet policy which began in 1985.

3

1985–90: TOWARDS A COMPREHENSIVE EASTERN POLICY FOR THE COMMUNITY

The Comecon summit meeting in June 1984 expressed its interest in a relationship with the Community. But it did so in terms that indicated no change of policy: readiness to conclude 'an appropriate agreement' between the two groups, in order to promote trade and economic relations.[1] Another wearisome phase appeared to be in prospect, with Comecon demands to negotiate as a group about trade and Community insistence that trade negotiations had to be with Comecon's member states. But October brought something new: a communication from Comecon to the Community suggesting negotiations for an agreement, declaration or other document. For the first time, Comecon conceded that negotiations did not have to result in an agreement covering trade.[2]

EC–Comecon: joint declaration and parallel approach
While the Community was digesting this new development, Mikhail Gorbachev replaced Konstantin Chernenko as secretary general of the Soviet communist party. When Prime Minister Bettino Craxi, President of the European Council during Italy's presidency of the Community during the first half of 1985, visited Moscow in May of that year, Gorbachev said that it was time not only to organize 'mutually advantageous relations' in economic matters – again nothing new – but also to 'seek a common language' on political matters to the extent that EC member states act as a 'political entity'.[3] This recognition of its political role presaged a new Soviet policy towards the Community, in line with the new international policy reflected in Gorbachev's summit meetings

with President Reagan, the arms control agreements and the acceptance of autonomy for the East Europeans. In June the secretary general of Comecon wrote to the President of the Commission proposing a joint declaration; and in September he sent a draft. This was short and simple, evidently seeking a first step in establishing relations without causing complications. It provided for official relations between the two groups 'in the context of their respective competences', which was interpreted as acceptance that trade negotiations would be a matter for Comecon's member states, since Comecon itself lacked explicit trade competence.[4] Beyond that, representatives of the two groups would meet to discuss the forms and methods of their relations and what areas they would cover.

The declaration was in principle acceptable to the Community provided it was clearly understood that such normal relations between the two groups would be accompanied by a normalization of bilateral relations between the Community and Comecon's member states. These states would, for example, accredit missions to the Community, as most other states throughout the world had done; they would negotiate trade agreements with the Community; and they would cease to oppose the representation of the Community in international organizations.[5] In February 1986, the Commissioner responsible for external relations, Willy De Clercq, wrote to Comecon and all its European member states, explaining the Community's policy; and by May all of them had replied accepting the parallel approach towards normal relations both between the two groups and among the Community and the Comecon member states.

Negotiations between the Community and Comecon began in September 1986. But, despite the simplicity of the draft declaration, they proceeded slowly. There were two reasons for this. First, the Community wanted to be sure that the Comecon states would indeed normalize bilateral relations before it concluded the declaration establishing relations with Comecon itself: it wanted to see sufficient progress with bilateral trade negotiations. Second, on the Soviet side there was reluctance to accept the 'territorial clause' that would make it clear that the writ of the Community also ran in West Berlin. Eventually, in May 1988, the Soviet Union, and hence Comecon, accepted a text containing the 'Hungarian formula', which did not mention Berlin but noted that the agreement would apply with respect to those areas in which the EEC Treaty was applicable. This formula, which was first devised in 1978 for an agreement between the Community and Hungary on trade in textiles, was but one example of the usefulness of a technical precedent when there is the political will to find a solution.

The joint declaration, signed at Luxembourg on 25 June 1988, provided for official relations between the Community and Comecon; for cooperation between them on matters of mutual interest; and for subsequent agreement on the fields, forms and methods of such cooperation. Much negotiation about very little, it may be thought. The relationship between the Community and Comecon has indeed come to almost nothing as the significance of Comecon has faded away. But the Community's insistence on bilateral trade negotiations with the eastern countries did bear fruit. The Community concluded the first trade agreement with Hungary only three months after the joint declaration with Comecon had been signed, and by October 1990 agreements had been concluded with all of Comecon's European member states. Although not in themselves important, the agreements have offered a starting point for the deepening of relations with these states, and in particular for the Europe Agreements that are to enter into force with Czechoslovakia, Hungary and Poland in 1992.

Trade and cooperation agreements
The Community's first trade and cooperation agreement with a Comecon country, Hungary, entered into force in December 1988; and the second, with Poland, in December 1989.[6] This was followed by one with the Soviet Union, in force from April 1990. Czechoslovakia had concluded a trade agreement in December 1988, not yet meriting the element of 'cooperation' owing to its regime's stubborn resistance to reform; but after the free elections this was replaced by a trade and cooperation agreement effective, like that with Bulgaria, from November 1990. Romania's trade and cooperation agreement, to replace its trade agreements of 1980, was finally signed in October 1990, but the Community delayed its enactment until Romania had responded adequately to its protests against the violent repression in June 1990; and the agreement did not enter into force until March 1991. The government of the GDR, once Erich Honecker had been ousted in November 1989, asked the Community for a trade and cooperation agreement; and this had reached the point of being initialled in the record time of less than four months.[7] But it was overtaken by German unification, and hence by eastern Germany's entry into the Community, before it had time to become effective. Yugoslavia, having been rewarded for its independence from the Soviet bloc with the trade and cooperation agreement of 1980, remained with that agreement, but from 1987 a new financial protocol was added,

envisaging loans of up to ecu 550 million from the European Investment Bank for Yugoslav infrastructure in the period to mid-1991.

These trade and cooperation agreements had much in common. All were for ten years, save that with Poland, which was for five years. Much of the significance of these periods was overtaken by the more advanced arrangements made in 1990. Not only did the eastern part of Germany join the Federal Republic and thus the Community. The Community also granted all except the Soviet Union much greater concessions on tariffs and quotas unilaterally than it had negotiated into the bilateral agreements; and it decided to offer more far-reaching association, first to Czechoslovakia, Hungary and Poland, and then to other countries that should make similar progress towards democratic and economic reform. But the agreements are still worth examining. That with the Soviet Union is still the basis for the relationship in practice as well as by contract; and the contractual relationship with the other countries will continue to stand should the Community withdraw its unilateral concessions, whether because any of them should fail to make the necessary progress with reforms or for any other reason.

In their provision for the regulation of trade, the agreements covered all goods save those for which the Community's responsibility stems from the Treaty establishing the European Coal and Steel Community (ECSC). This was, for the Community, a neat way of placing off-limits its special regime for steel and its protection against Polish coal. For textiles, which come under the EEC Treaty, the same device was not possible; but it was made clear that the textile quotas under the Multi-Fibre Arrangement would not be affected by the new agreements. For agricultural products, the Community granted Poland some reductions of tariffs and levies, gaining some reciprocal tariff reductions in return; the agreements with Czechoslovakia, Hungary and Romania did not provide for specific reciprocation in this field, but left it to be considered in the joint committees that were set up to oversee the working of each trade and cooperation agreement.

For all products covered by the agreements, the principle of the most-favoured nation (mfn) was to apply, although in a way that lacked much practical significance. The Community's partners were not to discriminate against economic agents originating in the Community in matters of trade. But the members of the Gatt, that is Bulgaria, Czechoslovakia, Hungary, Poland, Romania and Yugoslavia, were already committed to this; and the Soviet Union, unless and until it is ready to accede to the Gatt, is likely to retain an economy of a kind that makes it hard to establish whether there has been discrimination on account of a firm's origin. The Community itself was already committed to mfn treatment of tariffs on imports from the Gatt members, and has in practice always applied it to the others. So as regards mfn treatment of tariffs, they have had no problem with the Community – except of course that most-favoured nations have in fact become a small group of least-favoured nations, since the Community has given preferences to almost all other countries save Australia, Canada, Japan, New Zealand, South Africa and the United States. As regards tariffs, then, the only change in mfn status was that the Community is now contractually bound to apply to imports from the Soviet Union the tariff status that it has in fact always applied in the past.

For import quotas, the Community had never applied the mfn principle to its trade with Comecon countries. When Hungary, Poland and Romania joined the Gatt, the western countries insisted on protocols to legitimate the specific quotas they had applied to imports from state-trading countries. The trade and cooperation agreements with these countries provided that the protocols could continue to apply; and agreements with the others specified similar limits to mfn treatment. But the agreements also set a term to this discrimination. The main objective of the Hungarians when they negotiated the first of the trade and cooperation agreements with a Comecon country was indeed to secure an end to the specific quotas. It has been argued that they affected only a small proportion of the Comecon exports to the Community.[8] But the incidence on their exports of manufactures was higher; and the removal of the quotas would enable those exports to increase. So the Hungarians attached more importance to this aim than the proportion of the existing exports limited by these quotas may have appeared to justify. They eventually won their point, even if the argument about it helped to spin the negotiations out for nearly two years. The agreement provided for the elimination by the end of 1995 of the specific quotas, as distinct from the 'non-specific' quotas on imports of items that were restricted without specific discrimination against state-trading countries, the most significant being steel, textiles and agricultural products. Czechoslovakia and Poland, whose agreements were completed after they had moved far towards reform, were accorded an earlier date, the end of 1994. But Bulgaria, Romania and the Soviet Union, which, like Hungary when its agreement was concluded, had less convincing reform credentials, were likewise given 1995. The Community divided the process of quota removal into phases, moving from the less to the more sensitive products; and each agreement provided for a review by the end of 1992 which could lead to earlier liberalization.

Behind the quotas, as a further line of defence, the Community retained its right to apply safeguards, that is protective measures, usually again quotas, if, as the Gatt puts it, a product is imported 'so as to cause or threaten serious injury' to domestic producers. The Community has seldom in recent years imposed safeguards as such; but it has fairly frequently secured the consent of countries exporting to it too successfully to apply Voluntary Restraint Agreements (VRAs), which the exporting countries are inclined to accept because they know that the alternative is a safeguard measure, which may be harder to remove. The Hungarians had to pay for being the first to secure a date for the elimination of specific quotas by accepting a reinforced safeguard clause to last until 1998. This, like other such anomalies, is due for removal under Hungary's Europe Agreement. But the Community is still wedded to the concept of safeguards as a defence against too-successful exporters from its neighbours to the East.

The main substance of the trade part of these agreements was, then, the programmes for removing the Community's quotas, qualified by the continued availability of safeguards. The substance of the part that goes under the name of cooperation was less definite. The aim was to encourage trade and economic relations by means that go beyond traditional trade policy. This was to include the organization of events such as exhibitions, fairs and conferences, and the exchange of commercial information.

The agreements also listed fields in which cooperation was envisaged, usually because the eastern partners hoped to gain something by listing them. Thus for Czechoslovakia the list contained technical assistance to structural adjustment, including the tertiary sector and the conversion of arms production to civilian production; education and vocational training; and health and the environment, especially pollution and nuclear plants. The Romanians were interested in agriculture, tourism, financial services, environment, health, cooperatives, small companies and privatization. The Soviet list included banking and insurance, transport, tourism, other services, environment, management and vocational training, joint ventures, small and medium enterprises, science and technology – nuclear research, specified among the latter, being one of the fields in which the Community itself identified an interest in cooperation.

But it is doubtful how much these lists would mean without finance to pay for the cooperation; and unlike the Community's agreements with Mediterranean countries, in which the Community undertakes to provide such money, the member states ensured that no such money was to be offered under the Community's agreements with the Comecon countries. Not that there was any objection to the principle of providing finance to these countries. Far from it. The member states provided large sums in the context of their own cooperation agreements, which were to continue running in parallel with the Community's trade and cooperation agreements; and the member governments safeguarded their right to do this by having the 'Canada clause' inserted into the Community's agreements, thus denoted because the first such clause appeared in a cooperation agreement concluded with Canada in 1976. Britain, France, Germany and Italy were particularly insistent on this; and the juridical basis for it was sought by concluding the agreements not only under article 113 EEC, which gives the Community its exclusive competence in commercial policy, but also under article 235, which allows the Council, voting unanimously, to take measures if this 'should prove necessary to attain in the course of the operation of the common market, one of the objectives of the Community and this Treaty has not provided the necessary powers'. The member governments held that this would help to justify their parallel activities under their cooperation agreements.[9]

Without finance, the cooperation parts of the Community's agreements had little substance. The Community sought guarantees of non-discrimination in the granting of licences for imports from the Community, as well as the allocation of foreign exchange for such licensed imports and in connection with investments by Community firms; and it got the eastern countries to agree that export prices would conform to market prices, thus preventing market disruption by goods that were subsidized or priced irrationally under the command-administrative systems – even if this would also prevent the eastern countries from reaping the benefit of comparative advantage where they might have it. The eastern partners could count their gains in reducing the Community's import protection and hope that the cooperation provisions would come to something. But, even if the trade provisions were unexciting and if the cooperation may not amount to much, the agreements confirmed that the new phase of relations with the Comecon countries which began in 1985 could produce a practical result – long delayed by the Soviet refusal to deal with the Community, but now a useful first step.

For Central Europeans, these first steps were soon surpassed as a result of the extraordinary events of 1989 and 1990: the liberalization in

Poland and Hungary; the fall of Erich Honecker in October 1989; and the rapid transition to democracy in Czechoslovakia. The Community responded to these events with a remarkable transformation of its policies.

From 1989: a new phase of Community policy

Already in December 1988, the European Council of heads of state and government, meeting in Rhodes, saw the need for the Community to respond to the increasing opportunities for freedom in the Soviet bloc, reflected in the improved results of the CSCE process; and it reinforced this priority at its meeting in Madrid in June 1989. When the summit of G7, the Group of Seven major industrialized countries, met in Paris in July, the Community was poised to accept the invitation to the Commission to coordinate the actions of the Group of 24 OECD countries (G24) in the PHARE (Poland and Hungary: aid for economic reconstruction) programme of aid to help Poland and Hungary carry through their reforms. Then the Community's move towards a new policy was given a tremendous impulse by the liberalization in East Germany. In its determination to secure a favourable context for German unification and for the future of the unified German state, the Federal Republic became a powerful protagonist of a policy to promote the transition to democracy and a market economy in Central Europe and, as far as possible, in the rest of Eastern Europe, and to contribute to stability in the area. Britain, France and Italy likewise promoted such a policy and other member states supported it; so the way was open to move towards a comprehensive eastern policy for the Community with aid as well as trade among its major elements.

Emergency aid was given to Poland in the winter of 1989/90, following the example of 1983, when food and medical supplies were provided in order to avert the danger of hunger during that difficult time; and food aid has since been granted to Bulgaria, Romania and the Soviet Union. But the main aim of aid under the PHARE programme is to support the process of reform in the recipient countries. The total sum allocated for this in the Community budget for 1990 was ecu 500 million: ecu 300 million for Hungary and Poland (one-third for the former, two-thirds for the latter), allocated before the end of 1989; then another ecu 200 million for other East European countries, which was added to the budget during 1990 when it became clear how reform was spreading through the area. The connection with democratic and market reforms was explicit. The Commission stressed the importance of the 'basic legislation needed to move towards democratic and competitive market-orientated economic systems', and held, in May 1990, that 'the infrastructure of political and reform programmes' had 'largely satisfied the conditions for the extension of coordinated assistance' that had been approved by the G24 at its meeting on 13 December 1989.[10] In 1990, the Community committed itself to allocate ecu 850 million in 1991 and ecu 1 billion in 1992.

This money from the Community's budget takes the form of grants. The Community's institutions had also, by January 1991, provided ecu 2 billion of loans; and the member governments had allocated ecu 1.6 billion of grants and ecu 4.9 billion of loans,[11] apart from their contributions through the World Bank, the IMF and the European Bank for Reconstruction and Development (BERD – the French initials, which are more pronounceable than the English ones) which was launched on their initiative.

While the Community and its member states are the largest contributors to the BERD and to the PHARE programme as a whole, they are joined in it by the US and Japan and other western countries, as well as by the international institutions. But although the aid – which is analysed in Chapter 7 – is already on a considerable scale, with some ecu 6 billion in grants and ecu 14 billion in loans pledged by the end of January 1991, together with the ecu 10 billion of capital for the BERD, it may be less important for the East European economies than the opening of the Community market to their exports. Also in the context of the PHARE programme, the Community went far to liberalize its imports, first from Hungary and Poland, then from Bulgaria, Czechoslovakia and Romania, bringing them to the level of liberalization already enjoyed by Yugoslavia. From January 1990 it accorded Hungary and Poland the Generalized System of Preferences (GSP), which provides tariff-free access for manufactures, subject to quotas beyond which the tariff is applied on a number of sensitive products. This was extended in October to Bulgaria and Czechoslovakia; and, in January 1991, the more limited version previously granted to Romania was upgraded to be on a par with those of the others. The GSP includes textiles and some agricultural products but not coal and steel, and, for Poland, it virtually excludes fish, which has been subject to a separate negotiation between Poland and the Community. Poland was, however, allowed to suspend the tariff cuts on imports of some agricultural products from the Community which it had conceded, for the sake of reciprocity, in its trade and cooperation agreement.[12]

Despite the limits to the tariff-free access on sensitive products – which are, of course, those for which the suppliers are particularly competitive – the GSP is a major benefit for these countries. On top of this, quotas were liberalized on imports into the Community, initially, like the GSP, from Hungary and Poland, and then from Bulgaria, Czechoslovakia and Romania. All the specific quotas were eliminated; and non-specific quotas, with the important exceptions of those for coal, steel, textiles and most of the agricultural products to which they apply, have been suspended until the end of 1991. Some member states had imposed such quotas on a number of products, including for example footwear and some consumer electronics, and these were removed from the imports from East European countries. The suspension may be renewed for further years, although for Czechoslovakia, Hungary and Poland this is overtaken by the more far-reaching Europe Agreements. Looking further ahead, the Commission indicated that the GSP was likely to remain in place for East Europeans for some five years, 'while they are engaged in restructuring their economies'; but this too has been overtaken for Central Europeans by the Europe Agreements.[13] The combination of GSP, removal of specific quotas and suspension of non-specific quotas makes the Community's concessions under the trade and cooperation agreements look modest in comparison, giving other East Europeans privileges that Yugoslavia had acquired over the years with its GSP and other advantages that were secured through its agreement under the Community's Mediterranean policy.

Towards a comprehensive eastern policy for the Community
Since the Community embarked on its common commercial policy in 1974, political as well as economic motives have been important in its policy towards its neighbours to the East. A motive for refusing to respond to Comecon's proposals to deal as a group with the Community on trade policy was to resist the extension of the Soviet Union's hegemony over the external trade of other Comecon countries; and the agreements and GSP accorded to Romania and Yugoslavia were rewards for their independent policies. Disapproval of the Soviet intervention in Afghanistan was a motive for suspending the talks with Comecon in 1979; and the martial law in Poland, seen as an act of Soviet policy, provoked the modest sanctions against the Soviet Union in 1982. During the negotiation of trade agreements and of trade and cooperation agreements since 1985, the Community constantly differentiated among the eastern partners on political grounds.[14]

Thus the agreement concluded with Czechoslovakia in December

1988 was only a trade agreement, while in the same month the trade and cooperation agreement with Hungary entered into force, recognizing the progress towards economic reform as well as political liberalization; and the replacement of the trade agreement by a trade and cooperation agreement with Czechoslovakia followed the free elections there in March 1990. Negotiations with Bulgaria were suspended from May 1989 to March 1990 because of the infringement of rights of the Turkish minority. The negotiations with Romania proceeded with stops and starts. Negotiations to replace the 1980 trade agreements by a trade and cooperation agreement started in April 1987. They were suspended in July 1989 following violent repression by Ceausescu; and, just before the demise of Ceausescu in December 1989, the Committee of Permanent Representatives of the Community's member states (Coreper) decided that Romania's GSP and its 1980 trade agreements should be suspended, although before the Community could act on the idea, Ceausescu was no more.[15] The negotiations were restarted in May 1990 following the elections in that month; reached the point of initialling an agreement in June, before the violent repression later that month by the new regime; and arrived at signature in October, but with the Community reserving its formal conclusion of the agreement until there should be enough progress towards democracy and economic reform. Technical assistance under the PHARE programme was also delayed, until the Romanian government and opposition sent their reports on the evidence about the June events to the European Parliament and the Commission in January 1991, whereupon the G24 decided that the aid should start to flow. The Community at the same time accepted that the trade and cooperation agreement could go ahead and it entered into force in March.

All these differences among the negotiations and agreements with the East European countries were politically motivated. The more powerful policy instruments that were brought into play from the beginning of 1990 in response to democratic and market reforms were clearly, and usually explicitly, intended to support the prospects for the success of the reforms, and discriminated in favour of the countries that were judged to have the most credible reform programmes. This was true of the aid under the PHARE programme, of the GSP and the removal of quotas in 1990, and of the aims of BERD as set down in its statutes; and it was explicit in the Commission's Communication to the Council and Parliament proposing Europe Agreements with Czechoslovakia, Hungary, Poland and eventually other countries.[16] The Soviet Union, where reforms had not been judged ripe for a response on such a scale, appeared to be making such progress in 1990 that the European Council decided, in December, that the Community should go beyond its trade and co-operation agreement to a more comprehensive and important agreement to develop EC-Soviet relations and should meanwhile offer the Soviet Union substantial food aid and technical assistance – although events in the Baltic republics and setbacks to the reform process were soon to raise doubts about how far and how fast this policy should be pursued. But, on the whole, with this use of more powerful instruments in favour of pluralist polities and economies, the Community took a major step towards a common foreign policy with respect to its eastern neighbours.

This movement towards a common foreign policy, to which the member states were committed by article 30.1 of the Single European Act (SEA), required a closer coordination than had hitherto been normal between the general foreign policy cooperation sought under the system of European Political Cooperation (EPC) and the use of the Community's instruments of external economic policy under its common commercial policy. Soon after the Rhodes meeting of the European Council, which had underlined the importance of the Community's relations with the countries to the East, the Belgian government pressed for the Community to formulate a coherent and global view of its policy in this field.[17] The exchange of information between the EPC and Coreper, whose concern was to prepare for the Council's decisions on the economic aspects of external policy, was improved; and, for the Madrid meeting of the European Council in June 1989, a paper on policy towards the East was prepared jointly by the Spanish presidency, the Commission and the EPC secretariat.[18] The European Council concluded that it was necessary to integrate the political and economic aspects of Community policy in this field.

The coordination of Community institutions is a complex business. The relationship between the EPC and Coreper has already been mentioned. These two should provide the channels for coordination of the Community's policies with those of the member states, although such coordination is far from perfect. Then these intergovernmental bodies have to work with the Commission, which has always been the case for Coreper but is a fairly new requirement for EPC. The Commission itself has two directorates general heavily involved in policy towards the East: DG I, responsible for external relations and hence for trade, or trade and cooperation, agreements, for association and for the PHARE programme, in particular the technical assistance; and DG II, responsible for economic and financial affairs and thus for the macroeconomic input to

PHARE, in particular the financial assistance, and for studies of the eastern partners' economies. To this must be added inputs from the directorates general for agriculture; credit and investments; development; energy; enterprise policy; environment; internal market and industrial affairs; regional policy; science, research and development; telecommunications, information industries and innovation. The Economic and Social Committee is consulted on certain aspects; and the European Parliament, in addition to its consultative role, has certain powers of decision.

The European Parliament has long shown a lively interest in policy towards the East.[19] It has produced a string of reports on various aspects of the subject.[20] In December 1985, soon after the opportunity to resume negotiations between the Community and Comecon became evident, the socialist group of the European Parliament sent a delegation to Moscow, followed by one from the Christian Democrats, and then by a delegation of Soviet parliamentarians to the European Parliament. In January 1987, the Parliament itself decided to establish three new interparliamentary delegations: one for the Soviet Union; one for Central European countries; and one for other East Europeans.

The European Parliament has a power of codecision with the Council for the Community's budget. Although this power is attenuated in relation to the agricultural part of the budget and a few other headings, it applies to the grants for the PHARE programme and the Soviet Union. In drawing up the budget for 1990, the Council and the Commission agreed on ecu 200 million as the sum to be allocated for aid to Hungary and Poland. But the Parliament raised this to ecu 300 million, which was accepted by the other institutions. In addition to the budgetary codecision, the SEA gave the Parliament powers over association with the Community and accession to it, under what is called the assent procedure. Article 9 SEA, amending article 236 EEC, requires the assent of the Parliament before the Council can conclude an association agreement; and article 8 SEA, amending article 235 EEC, requires the Parliament's assent before the Council can act on an application for membership. The power over association agreements brings with it the need for coordination between the Parliament and the Commission and Council with respect to the negotiation of such agreements.

The powers of the EC and the relationship among its institutions are not static. The powers have been increased and the institutional relationships adjusted in a number of significant steps to bring the Community to where it is today.[21] The Intergovernmental Conferences (IGCs) that opened in December 1990 are intended to result in further such steps, which may affect the future of policy towards Eastern Europe. Thus the IGC on economic and monetary union is likely to accord the Community monetary powers that may enhance the content of its relationships with these countries. One motive for the convening of the IGC on political union was to strengthen the Community as a framework to contain the united German state;[22] and this could imply more majority voting in the Council and a stronger role for the European Parliament with respect to at least some aspects of Community policy towards the East. The governments of some member states feared that if this was not done, Germany would come to pursue an increasingly independent policy, thus weakening the Community and bringing instability into the relationships of the Germans and their Community partners, and hence into Europe as a whole. A positive outcome for the IGCs could, on the other hand, reinforce the Community's capacity to pursue an effective policy towards the East, and to make a more powerful contribution to the Europe Agreements with Central European countries in particular.

4

IMPLICATIONS OF EASTERN REFORMS FOR WESTERN POLICIES

The European Community, with its western partners, favours pluralist democracy and market economy in its neighbours to the East. These are the aims of the Community in negotiating association agreements with the Central European countries and of the PHARE programme comprising the G24 aid to Eastern Europe.[1] Movement in the same direction in the Soviet Union is likewise strongly in the Community's interest. The questions for policy are on what conditions, how, and on what scale the western countries, and the Community in particular, can contribute to these ends.

The Community can help to develop and open the eastern economies through its trade and cooperation agreements and through technical assistance, on condition that the eastern governments maintain neither an unacceptable political stance nor an economic policy that negates the Community's concessions. Once a reforming East European country has a credible programme to create a market economy and pluralist democracy, the Community can commit itself to the deeper relationship of a Europe Agreement and to more comprehensive aid; and the Community will subsequently wish to reassure itself that the programme is proceeding successfully. Such countries can become valid candidates for accession to the Community when pluralist democracy and a competitive market economy are securely established. The decisions to move from one stage to the next are of great political significance. They should be based on careful judgments about the progress and prospects of both political and economic reforms. The Community needs the intellectual framework and the professional and political skills to judge as soundly as possible. It also needs to direct its trade and aid policies to give the most effective support to appropriate reform. Much has recently been written about the reforms.[2] The aim of this chapter is merely to consider some of the criteria on which the Community's judgments should be based.

CREATING PLURALIST DEMOCRACIES

Free and multi-party elections are a first test of the intention to move towards pluralist democracy. But they are far from sufficient, as events after the elections in Romania in 1990 were soon to demonstrate. Representative government and the rule of law based on human rights have to become firmly established; and this requires a complex infrastructure of political and civil institutions and behaviour. Negotiations for the association of Central European countries with the Community were opened on the assumption that these conditions would be met there; the opening of negotiations with Yugoslavia would, the Commission proposed in its Communication on Europe Agreements, depend on its 'fulfilment of commitments to reform'; and the situation in Bulgaria and Romania would be monitored until the necessary conditions were established.[3] But there has been surprisingly little public discussion about the political conditions for association, or about the elements of pluralist democracy that association and aid are intended to encourage.

The elements of political reform

Multi-party elections are not sufficient, but they are certainly necessary. They should be broadly even-handed among different parties, which does not come easily where, as in the Balkans, history or civil society has not thrown up strong autonomous movements which can challenge a party that has long monopolized power. Elections cannot be regarded as satisfactory until such parties have a good chance of winning them. Nor will the parliaments be genuine elements of pluralist democracy until they have real power to enact legislation and to control the executive, which depends partly on the constitution and partly on the capacity of the parliament's members and staff.

The quality of MPs depends, in turn, on the quality of the parties from which they come. These require the capacity to make policies and programmes; to relate to the public and fight elections effectively; and, in addition to producing competent MPs, to produce, for the parliamentary executives that characterize most European states, ministers able to form responsible governments. The government in such a system must be dismissible by the parliament, preferably with safeguards to prevent unstable government; alternatively, it can in a presidential system be dismissible by the voters direct. In either case it must, like the citizens, be subject to the rule of law, applied by independent courts dedicated to uphold human rights as well as to interpret the law in general; and this depends not just on the judges but also on a competent legal profession.

Nor will such a government work without a competent civil service, able to serve governments composed by whichever democratic parties may win the elections. Reaching further into the society, this principle has to apply to education and to the economy: both must shake free of the habit of domination by a monopoly party. If the principle's application is widened further again, it becomes that of the civil society, based, within the rule of law, on 'the autonomy of private associations and institutions', including private business firms.[4] Of particular significance for the political process are the independence and quality of the media.

All these elements may be taken for granted when the aim of democracy is stated. But, unless they are spelt out, it may not be evident what profound and many-sided change is required of countries moving from a marxist-leninist party power monopoly to a stable pluralist democracy. There, the 'leading role of the party' has been a euphemism for pervasive control of the polity, economy and society: of the government, armed forces, police and often a 'workers' militia; of the administration and the courts; of the management of economic and social organizations; of the media, education and the arts. The party has narrowed the space for civil society as far as it could. The constituent republics, in purportedly federal states, have been controlled by the monopolistic party, not through the rule of law and a democratic political process as in a genuine federation. Citizens, organizations and republics have been denied the opportunity to exercise independent responsibility, and may have forgone some of the capacity to do so.

Under the euphemism of 'democratic centralism', the party itself has been controlled by a small group at the centre, often by one man. The centre has squeezed the civil society through its domination of the party, reaching out through the nomenklatura, which comprises almost all influential people, and through its control over people's jobs, all backed by the centre's control over the party's vast property, access to state resources and, last but not least, the secret police.[5]

'Proletarian internationalism' was the euphemism for the projection of the 'leading role' of the Communist Party of the Soviet Union onto the international stage. Thus the centre of the Soviet Party controlled the East

Europeans: Stalin's bequest, formalized in the Brezhnev doctrine. Thus also, the centre promoted international struggle against 'bourgeois' rule and capitalism: that is to say, against pluralist democracy and the market economy.

It is the vast and complex process of transition from this monopoly of political power to pluralist democracy that has to be studied and assessed if the Community and the G24 are to further their stated aim of helping the transition.

Political reform in Eastern Europe

Czechoslovakia, Hungary and Poland will have completed their first round of free and multi-party elections after the Polish parliamentary elections of 1991. The elections have been on the whole remarkably successful, despite low turnouts by voters in some of them.

But, although the new political forces in each country proved strong enough to beat the communists, the future success of the multi-party system cannot be taken for granted. Czechoslovakia and Poland have yet to establish that the new parties replacing Civic Forum and Solidarity, which provided united fronts against the old regimes, will ensure viable multi-party systems. The Hungarian parties have not yet acquired stable bases of support among the voters. In each country a significant minority has voted for the old communist parties (if under new names), reaching as many as 14% in the Czechoslovak elections of June 1990. Thus these parties have retained a base from which they might revive, particularly if the economic reforms should fail. But, if political or economic reforms do not succeed, a communist revival is less likely than the emergence of authoritarian nationalist regimes.[6] Such failure could also cause Slovak nationalists to split the Czech and Slovak Federal Republic.[7]

The government in each case marks a clear break with the past; nor have complaints been heard that the old habits continue to pollute the judicial institutions. But there has been unease at the continuing prevalence of people who comprised the nomenklatura. That may be inevitable, since they include most of the qualified administrators and many of the managers and professional people; and many of them are doubtless ready to play their due part in the new system. But such unease was one cause of Lech Walesa's success in forcing the holding of the Polish presidential elections in 1990; and the start of the programme of privatization in Czechoslovakia has been clouded by resentment against those with the wealth to bid the prices of small businesses up, some of such bidders being former members of the nomenklatura who have 'done well out of the class war'. It is to be hoped that enough citizens will have been convinced by the robust argument of the minister in charge of privatization: 'the best way to clean dirty money is to let it work for the people. Let it be invested.'[8]

Each of the three countries has a substantial base for civil society. In Poland, samizdat and relatively free speech have long been tolerated; and the communists were confronted by the Church and, for the past decade, Solidarity as countervailing social forces. In Czechoslovakia, despite the repressive regime, the Charter 77 group could build on a democratic tradition, which had made itself felt again in 1968. In Hungary, after the people had shown the limits of their tolerance in 1956, János Kádár changed the balance between party and civil society with the slogan 'he who is not against us is with us': despite the limitation implied for active opposition, this did permit more latitude for different opinions in writing, discussing, teaching and holding jobs. Since 1989, it has not been so hard for these countries to produce a free press, although there may still be room for doubt whether the long repression has not caused the capacity for criticism to outrun that for responsible judgment and action.

The Community was right to negotiate for Europe Agreements with these countries on the grounds that they are launched on the way towards pluralist democracy. But stable democracy is not a *fait accompli*. Economic failure or the rise of destructive nationalism could reverse the process. The Community should study carefully where and how assistance could be applied to help consolidate the process of transition. A thoroughly worked out and adequate aid programme is needed, not only for the economic transition, but also to strengthen the elements of pluralist democracy such as those outlined above.

Yugoslavia presents a harder problem, although the constraints that the communist regime placed on civil society were for decades less severe than in other parts of Eastern Europe. There was more freedom of expression and greater use of market mechanisms in the economy, and it was not so surprising when the League of Communists decided to allow multi-party elections in the republics in 1990. In four of the six republics, these elections produced governments composed of the new parties. But in Serbia, with one-third of the population of Yugoslavia, the communists won the elections, led by Slobodan Milosevic who was exploiting Serb nationalism. All-Yugoslav elections were not held in 1990 and the Yugoslav government remained the product of the old system, although the prime minister, Ante Markovic, had made good progress in designing a reform of the financial system, without, however, adequately tackling the enterprise system, which was the other main barrier to the achievement of a market economy. But the republics frustrated the effort to reform.

The most glaring example of republican recalcitrance was the Serbian government's illegal procurement of a loan of dinars 18 billion ($1 billion) from the republic's bank, to finance hand-outs, such as pension increases and industrial subsidies, as a device for gaining public support in the run-up to the election late in 1990,[9] thus driving a coach and horses through the Yugoslav government's stabilization programme agreed with the IMF, and giving inflation a sharp new thrust. The reaction in Croatia and Slovenia was to prepare themselves more urgently to be ready to launch their own currencies. Other threats to the unity of the Yugoslav economy have included curbs on trade between republics. Such economic disintegration has reflected the political conflict between Croatia together with Slovenia, with their urge to convert the Yugoslav state into a confederation or to secede from it, and Serbia, backed by the Yugoslav army, which is also dominated by communists who want to maintain their power.

This conflict may confront the Community with very difficult political decisions. It may have to decide how far to back republics that have adopted the principles of pluralist democracy and market economy and wish to deal direct with the Community on matters of Community competence, and how far to maintain the existing links with Yugoslavia. Under the less pleasant scenarios, this involves not just economics and politics, but also choices with security implications; and this raises the question of whether the Community has the capacity to deal with matters of foreign policy and security that can be seen as corollaries of its economic power.

In Bulgaria and Romania, the elections of 1990 produced governments from the communist parties, even if these had been given new names. For the election that it won in March 1991, the Albanian party did not find it necessary to change its name. In none of these cases was the civil society strong enough to throw up parties that could defeat the existing rulers. In Bulgaria, however, the opposition had the strength to force the appointment of men who were not communists both as president and as prime minister of a coalition government that has shown a new orientation towards economic and political reforms as well as external policy. But Romanian society was too desperately ravaged by Ceausescu to allow for such promising achievements in the early period under the new government. The extent of the damage done by the Stasi in East Germany has now been revealed. Ceausescu's Securitate was probably yet more pervasive and terrible and may still be influential. Albania's Sigurimi is likewise feared, even if Ramiz Alia, Enver Hoxha's successor as leader of the communist party, had the flexibility to respond to strikes and demonstrations by consenting to the multi-party elections. Unless this trend is reversed, there is no reason why the Community should not negotiate a trade and cooperation agreement, should Albania want one. In its Communication on Europe Agreements, the Commission saw the need to monitor the situation in Bulgaria and Romania to assess whether the necessary conditions would be established.[10] This monitoring is likely to continue for some time, although Bulgaria in particular might surprise sceptics about the prospects for civil society in the Balkans. Meanwhile, so long as the regimes avoid flagrant violations of human rights, the Community can help lay the foundations for pluralist democracy by assistance that aims to strengthen the civil society and in particular its economic aspect, the market economy.

Political change in the Soviet Union

When Russians could express themselves freely, thanks to the policy of glasnost in the later 1980s, it soon became apparent that 70 years of repression had not removed their capacity to demonstrate some essential features of civil society. Not only did the media become lively and critical, but the Russians, and some of the other nationalities in the Soviet Union, showed their skill at 'improvising human institutions under great pressure and stress'.[11] The consequences in new political institutions were dramatic.

After elections had allowed representatives of new movements into the reformed parliamentary institutions of the Soviet Union – the Congress of People's Deputies and the Supreme Soviet – they engaged in remarkably free debate and ensured that the new legislative powers were used, if not always responsibly. The radicals who wanted progress towards pluralist democracy and the market economy made the running until late in 1990. The new movements also secured control of most of the parliaments of the republics, as well as providing leadership in the Russian one, and of many cities, including Moscow and Leningrad. The role of the communist party was much reduced. President Mikhail Gorbachev, allied with the radicals and with the acquiescence of docile party representatives, pushed through the Soviet legislature the

43

amendment to article 6 of the constitution and thus removed from the communist party its statutory monopoly of power. Independent trade unions mushroomed, challenging the party-dominated unions. The position of the party's workplace organizations was weakened and many were wound up, thus removing one of the party's effective means of control.[12] At the top level, Gorbachev effected the transfer of government power from the Politburo to the Presidency.

But the new powers of the Presidency did not make for effective government. The command-administrative system of economic management, which had depended for its functioning on party control and repression, became ineffective before the institutions of a market economy had been put in its place. Most of the republics' legislatures determined that their own laws would prevail over those of the Soviet Union, and many of the commands from the centre were ignored in the republics. The new Federation Council, containing the presidents of the republics and autonomous regions, did not resolve these conflicts. By the end of 1990, the system was failing to cope with economic crisis and nationalist separatism.

More than in Central Europe, the civil society may have been deformed by the long years of repression, on top of the centuries of tsarist absolutism, so as to have more capacity to throw up criticism than to exercise public responsibility; the institutions that embody physical power, the armed forces and the KGB, can still resist reforms, as can the powerful economic interests that stand to lose from reform, such as managers of the defence industries and of the collective farms. Gorbachev, when push turned to shove in the winter of 1990/91, backed down in their favour from his policy of support for the reformers, most of whom left his government. His dilemma reflected the unresolved conflicts between conservative authority and the civil society, and between the centre and the republics, which was embodied in the struggle for power between him and Boris Yeltsin. However the conflicts and the struggle may appear to be resolved in 1991, it is not possible to predict where the Soviet Union and the republics will find themselves over the medium or longer term on the spectra between authoritarian government and pluralist democracy, between command and market economy, between union and separation.

The European Community should be ready for any of these possibilities. It needs to have the capacity to evaluate developments, and the institutions and instruments to act on its evaluation. Meanwhile, it can support elements of progress towards strengthening civil society and market economy, wherever Soviet institutions make it possible to do so effectively; and it should be ready to deal with individual republics in so far as they have powers in the Community's fields of competence, and in particular to support those that move towards pluralist democracy.

CREATING MARKET ECONOMIES

The relationship between economic and political reform

It is doubtful whether a command economy is compatible with pluralist democracy. It has long been argued that a market economy is the economic aspect of civil society;[13] and there have been no examples of pluralist democracies with command economies. The converse does not apply, however: Spain, Chile, South Korea and Taiwan are among the examples of market economies that have functioned under authoritarian governments. These have been governments that tolerated a degree of freedom for entrepreneurs and managers, in the expectation that this would consolidate political stability by delivering economic welfare. But their expectations of political quiescence may be disappointed over the longer term. Tensions arise between the economic civil society and the authoritarian polity. Some of those who have enjoyed economic freedom find political servitude irksome; and the economic civil society generates an educated middle class and offers space on which political independence can be built. Such was the experience in the transition of the Iberian peninsula and of Chile to democracy; and such tensions have arisen in South Korea and Taiwan. While there is no proof that a market economy will lead eventually to pluralist democracy, there is further evidence in the fact that all of the world's most advanced economies are in such democracies.

The evidence seems good enough to conclude that support for the transition to market economies in Eastern Europe and the Soviet Union is not only in the economic interest of the Community, to secure the scope for expanding trade, but also in its political interest, because it is probable that the market economy will eventually be accompanied by pluralist democracy. There is no case for providing such support to regimes that will waste it, either through inability to manage or through a failure to reform the polity to the extent necessary to enable a market economy to function. But should one or more of the Community's eastern neighbours fail to manage a full transition to pluralist democracy, or should they revert to a more authoritarian regime that nevertheless tolerates economic freedoms and does not adopt a hostile stance, the Community ought still to be open to the idea of assisting the process of economic reform.

Support for the countries that are establishing pluralist democracies should, however, be the stronger. This is particularly important in the early stages, when lack of economic success may more readily be followed by public disillusion with democracy, or simply by inability to handle the complex political processes involved. It will be necessary to consider how far the Community, if it does not raise the present level of support, will be exposing its neighbours to this risk.

The elements of economic reform

There is a substantial literature about the process of economic reform and much current news about it.[14] But it is only too easy to forget what an enormous task the reformers have to accomplish. The communist parties' control over the command economy, the economic aspect of their 'leading role', has, with its manipulation from the centre, undermined the habits that make for an efficient economy: making what consumers want to buy; working effectively for a reward; applying new technologies and innovating; facing international competition. The system has deprived economic agents of the juridical and institutional framework for a competitive and dynamic economy. The framework and the habits have to be formed anew, and from the starting-point of an economy that is stagnant, is prey to suppressed inflation, concealed unemployment, and corruption, and generates environmental disaster.

Macroeconomic reform is well-trodden ground, the speciality of the IMF, although experience has to be adapted to the problem of breaking out of this particular cul-de-sac. Those who have to control money and credit must not only deal with vast quantities of cash and deposits waiting for goods to buy, of inter-firm credits obtained by the simple device of not paying other firms' bills, and of non-performing debts at banks,[15] but must also establish new sets of financial institutions. Not only must total budget deficits be cut at a time when the people are already suffering economic pain, but a whole system based on financing firms through subsidies has to be transformed. Externally, a labyrinth of protectionist controls has to be replaced by a single market-clearing exchange rate, moving to convertibility, in the first place for residents' current transactions, and without negating the effect through excessive tariffs, quotas or exchange controls. The new exchange rate, kept stable through an adjustable peg to a suitable currency or basket, provides an anchor for monetary policy as well as for price determination.[16] But on top of the painful adjustments of thus wrenching the economy away from the old regime, there has been the collapse of trade within Comecon, and most of these countries are crushed by debt. The West has been helping with support for the balance of payments, for convertibility and for easing the debt burden, as well as by opening markets to enable eastern countries to earn more hard currencies. But the success of macroeconomic reform also depends on sustaining public support in the reforming countries and on the supply response of their economies to the new conditions. The West may help to maintain the public support by means of aid for social security, in particular unemployment pay. But the fundamental requirement is for the eastern countries to develop a dynamic supply side; and that depends on structural reform.

A first element in structural reform is the legislative framework for a market economy: laws on ownership and property rights; company law, including the procedures for bankruptcy; labour law, concerning hiring and firing, the right to strike, procedures for settling disputes; competition law; taxation; the system of price and wage determination (deregulation being the principal instrument here); the collection of statistics; and many others, including in particular the legislation regarding external trade and foreign investment.

A second element is the reform of enterprise structures, away from the predominance of monopolies owned by the state, to a system based mainly on joint-stock companies, together with partnerships, cooperatives and family businesses. This process takes some time, and meanwhile the state-owned companies can, in some cases, be demerged, and should in any case be freed from the tutelage of industrial ministries, be given market-economy guidelines and have their state subsidies phased out. Of particular importance are the financial institutions that are the basis for capital markets. Western technical assistance can be helpful for all these purposes.

A third element is the physical structure for a competitive economy: industrial plant and equipment; infrastructure; the service sectors; to which must be added a clean environment. The Centre for Economic Policy Research has estimated the cost of all this investment at between $103 billion and $226 billion a year for the next few years for Bulgaria, Czechoslovakia, Hungary, Poland and Romania combined, where domestic private savings may make a minimal contribution.[17] If such sums are to be found, the participation of foreign private investment will have to be large. In addition to the access to western capital markets that is involved, such investment is the most efficient vehicle for transferring management and technological skills across frontiers. A strong flow is a key to success in

47

the eastern economies and will be the best evidence of success. But it faces many problems in the early stages of reform: political and economic risks; poor transport, communications and other infrastructure; lack of qualified people for the particular jobs to be done; bureaucracies that still cause difficulties. So the flow of foreign investment is not at first likely to be enough to inject the needed dynamism into the economy and start the benign circle of growth. Nor will it in any case be provided for public goods, such as roads and the cleaning of the environment, which the eastern countries themselves will be hard put to it to finance.

This points to the need for public support for such investment from the West and, as the economic power most closely concerned, from the Community in particular. While loans for such purposes could normally be on bankable terms, most of the eastern countries are unable to support an increase in their debt-service obligations over the short to medium term, so a substantial grant element is indicated. Here again, technical assistance can perform a useful function.

A fourth fundamental deficiency in the structure of the eastern economies is in human capital and attitudes. Technical assistance programmes can again help with teaching the necessary skills. Attitudes are less readily conveyed. Yet such essential attributes as entrepreneurship and high productivity depend on them. Foreign investment can certainly help. But that too depends on an attitude open enough to receive and benefit from it, just as the success of a market economy depends on acceptance of such features as private property, pay differentials, price rises where these are needed to reflect costs, and a risk of unemployment. Conversely, acceptance of such things beyond the short term may depend, in reforming countries, on a measure of early economic success; and this raises the question of the sequencing of various aspects of reform and its relationship to the showing of results.

Debate among economists has focused on a choice between a big bang and a more gradual reform.[18] Central to the big bang is a macroeconomic policy that will stop inflation, whether inflation that is open, as in Poland in 1989 and to a much lesser extent in Hungary, or is suppressed and manifested in shortages, as in Czechoslovakia. With hyperinflation as it was in Poland or Yugoslavia, there is scarcely a choice: it must be halted by monetary and budgetary stringency and the external balance corrected by devaluation. Convertibility at a realistic exchange rate is then the firmest anchor for a credible macroeconomic policy. But the result can only be high unemployment, lower production and depressed investment. The questions are how much and for how long?

The answers depend on the response to the new conditions from the supply side of the economy.

The supply-side response depends on the structure of the economy, and in particular on the transition from the command to the market economy. Essential elements of the legislative framework for the market economy can be enacted within a year or two, although it will be longer before the market economy functions properly within that framework. A crucial choice is the rate at which price and wage controls and subsidies are dismantled. It is technically possible to make a bonfire of them all at once; the constraints are the effects on inflation in an economy in which competitive markets are still the exception rather than the rule, and on a society in which many people are near the bread-line. Thus the Poles used wage controls and food subsidies as buffers to moderate the effect of their big bang; and so long as product markets are dominated by monopolies, these may use their freedom to fix their prices in ways that perpetuate inflation, unless macroeconomic policy prevents it by forcing the economy into stagnation. Hence the importance of reforming the structure of enterprises as quickly as possible. But that is easier said than done in economies where over nine-tenths of industry may consist of state monopolies, where the institutions of a capital market have to be created, and where the potential shareholders lack money and experience. Privatization can be accelerated by issuing vouchers free of charge to citizens, which they can exchange for shares, and by giving financial institutions a role in the control of companies, such as the great banks have in Germany, or the pension funds, insurance companies and unit trusts in Britain; but time will be required for such a system to effect sufficient change in the behaviour of enterprises. It is over the medium rather than the short term that a competitive market structure can come to predominate, even if a liberal import regime can introduce some competition meanwhile. The same applies to the creation of adequate physical structure and human capital in the economy.

From the short to the medium term, then, the enterprise structure is likely to induce inflationary pressure; and the same goes for the physical structure, where there will be bottlenecks that make for inflation as well as discourage investment. Shortages of skilled people may have similar effects; and attitudes may conduce to the use of market power in inflationary ways and of democratic power in ways that inhibit the reforms.

The magic of political freedom and the market economy may enable the people of reforming countries to ride over such difficulties, to reach macroeconomic stability and a dynamic economy, with investment rising and unemployment falling, within a couple of years. But it would be unwise not to recognize that this may not happen: that unemployment and inflationary pressures may remain high, with investment and growth suppressed, leading to a sense of economic failure and a loss of public support for the reforms. The result depends on unknowns, such as the speed with which competitive markets can be created, with which skills and attitudes can be developed to use the new opportunities effectively, and with which large-scale foreign investment can be induced to flow. We should admit that we do not know which outcome to expect.

This is not a reason to oppose the big-bang approach. We do not know what outcome to expect from a more gradual one either: the odds on success may be worse. But it surely a reason not to take success following the big bang for granted, and hence not to base western policies with respect to the removal of protection and the volume of aid on the assumption that a modest western effort will ensure success. It is also a reason not to be dogmatic about the size of the bang and, for example, the speed at which subsidies or price and wage controls are to be eliminated. If a reforming government wants to relax wage controls over a period of, say, two to three years before they are abolished; if it wishes to free prices over such a period, starting with sectors in which competition is better established; if it sets a similar programme for reducing subsidies to an acceptable level: these are choices that it is entitled to make. But such a government should, for its part, accept that the step-wise approach exposes it to the risk that special interests will oppose each step and may be able to undermine public support for the programme and sap the government's will. Successive tranches of aid to support such a programme must be conditional on the taking of the successive steps.

The western preference has been for the bigger bangs, and reforming countries have been encouraged to undertake them. But western governments have not been ready to take an adequate share of the responsibility for ensuring that this advice does not lead to failures that could have damaging consequences for the future of Europe. The western contribution to ensuring success could include commitment by the EC to a big bang of its own in the reduction of protection against imports of agricultural as well as industrial products from its eastern partners, and to aid for assisting the unemployed and for cleaning the environment and other forms of investment beyond the scale so far contemplated. How much is needed, for what purposes and in what form depends, like the Community's offers of association, on conditions in each eastern country and on its programme for reform.

Economic conditions and reform in Central Europe

The transition from command to market economy is causing pain. Table 4.1 shows that the net material product of Bulgaria, Poland and Romania fell by over one-tenth in 1990, cutting already low incomes.[19] An expanding informal economy that escapes the official statistics may have alleviated the pain; but sharp pain there must have been in those three countries, even if in Czechoslovakia and Hungary the informal economy may have offset a good part of their smaller falls in production. The situation in the Soviet Union, although official statistics show a decline of no more than 4% in 1990, has been deteriorating rapidly. Inflation was at a rate of over 5% a month in each country early in 1991; and although unemployment was still low, except in Poland and Yugoslavia, policies to control inflation combined with the breakdown of the old system were causing it to rise fast.

With prices rising by 640% during 1989, the new Polish government that followed the bankrupt communist regime had to take drastic action. It pegged the zloty to the dollar and pursued a macroeconomic policy designed to keep it pegged by means of tight money, a budget surplus, wage control and 'internal convertibility' for residents' current transactions. This was the biggest bang among the reforming countries, apart from the eastern German Länder, which were exposed directly to the regime of the Federal Republic. There, by the end of 1990, unemployment was over 7% and rising very fast, while industrial production was down by 28% in 1990 and falling fast.[20] A bang on that scale would hardly be possible without a protective political and social framework such as the Federal Republic provides. The Polish one was fierce enough, bringing unemployment up from 0.1% to 6% during the course of 1990, with forecasts that it may nearly double again to 2 million by the end of 1991, when consumption could still be 10–20% less than at the start of 1990.[21] While continued stringency has been necessary, with inflation again high and rising by the end of 1990, this must raise fears for the public's continued support of a government that has to inflict such hardship on a people who are already much poorer than their neighbours in Central Europe.[22]

For Czechoslovakia and Hungary, with the rise of prices from 1989 to 1990 in single figures, such a sudden shock was not inevitable. But Czechoslovakia has moved to internal convertibility in 1991 and Hungary proposes to do so in 1992. Both governments have been severe: the Czechoslovak budget balance was shifted from a deficit of 0.9% of GDP in 1989 to a surplus of 0.8% in 1990, while the Hungarians cut their

Table 4.1 Macroeconomic condition of Eastern Europe and the Soviet Union in 1990

| | Net material product: change from 1989 to 1990 (%) | Consumer price rises | | | Unemployed Dec 1990 (%) | Trade balance with developed market economies ($bn) | Net debt end 1990 ($bn) |
| | | 1990 over 1989 (%) | Over previous months | | | | |
			Average Aug-Dec 1990 (%)	Jan 1991 (%)			
Bulgaria	-13.6	19.3	7.0	13.6	1.8	-0.8	10.4
Czechoslovakia	-3.1	10.1	n.a.	25.8	1.0	-0.6	6.8
Hungary	-5.5	28.9	1.9	7.5	1.7	0.8	20.0
Poland	-13.0	585	4.6	12.7	6.1	3.2	43.4
Romania	-10.5	5.7	n.a.	9.2	1.3	-0.9	1.3
Yugoslavia	-7.6*	588	4.7	5.6	13.2	n.a.	16.7
Soviet Union	-4.0	5.3	n.a.	4-6	1.4	-4.8	54.6

Source: UN Economic Commission for Europe, *Economic Survey of Europe in 1990-1991*, New York, United Nations, 1991, Tables A1 and B1 (material product), 2.2.11 (consumer prices), 2.2.14 (unemployed), 3.3.8 (trade balance), 3.3.12 (debt, with the Yugoslav figure for total debt from *The Financial Times*, 6 February 1991).

*Gross material product

deficit between the two years from 3.2% to 0.1% of GDP.[23] Much of this was achieved by cutting subsidies, with a concomitant rise in prices. These were 25% higher in Czechoslovakia in January 1991 than in the preceding month, casting doubt on the official forecast that inflation would be no more than 30% in 1991 as a whole.[24] The Hungarians' expectation that inflation will rise to 35% in 1991 and then fall seems realistic, and creditably so, given the inflationary pressure that must result from servicing a debt which has been consuming about one-half of Hungary's earnings of hard currency.[25] The tight macroeconomic policy to counter inflation is expected to lead in both countries to declines of around 5% of GDP in 1991, although the growth of the private sector may offset at least some of that; and unemployment will rise in Czechoslovakia to an estimated 7–10% by the end of the year.[26]

The macroeconomic policies of all three Central European countries can be regarded as satisfactory in difficult circumstances. Concern about Poland must focus on its ability to prevent inflation from taking off again and at the same time to maintain enough public support to enable the government to continue its policy. For Czechoslovakia and Hungary, with their approach by steps rather than a big bang, the need is to persist with steps that not only attain convertibility but also maintain it with a stable exchange rate.

It is at the same time necessary to monitor the three economies for signs of dynamic growth, because both economic and political reform would fail if they were to be blighted by stagflation. In 1990, the trade surpluses with developed market economies, of $3.2 billion for Poland and $0.8 billion for Hungary, were encouraging, even if it will be hard to repeat the performance without the advantage of cheap energy and materials from Comecon. For Hungary the inflow of foreign investment amounted to $1 billion, with the total number of joint ventures rising to some 5,000 by the end of the year. Most of these were small, but are evidence of lively western interest. Poland, with its greater problems, received much less.[27] Czechoslovakia was powerfully backed by Volkswagen, with its purchase of a 79% stake in Skoda for DM 1.4 billion (ecu 0.7 billion), and commitment to an investment programme of DM 9 billion (ecu 4.5 billion) over the next ten years. Since few statistics are available for the domestic private sectors, which are at present the main domestic source of dynamic development, the Central Europeans' prospects for achieving healthy growth must be judged mainly by their progress with reforms to improve the structure of their economies. Four main elements of these reforms were listed earlier: the legislative framework, including liberalization of prices and of external economic relations; the enterprise structure; the physical structure; and human capital and attitudes.

Each of these three countries is making progress with the legislation for a market economy, though a good deal of time will be required in order to complete it. Prices are being freed at varying rates; if they are not substantially free by the end of 1991, it may be a sign that reform is faltering. Poland has opened itself to import competition with a low tariff at 9% weighted average, combined with convertibility. Hungary, with a tariff averaging some 13%, has removed almost all quota restrictions.[28] Legislation on property rights has proved difficult, with conflict between the claims of expropriated former owners to repossess, and the need of those buying property to be sure that they really do own it. Here again, clear and workable legislation is required in 1991.

Reform of the structure of enterprises is crucial to the whole reform process. Both Hungary and Poland already have a substantial private sector. In Poland, much of this comprises small farms that are not yet dynamic, though with the capacity to become so; but the number of new small businesses, mostly in the service sector, has run well into six figures since the arrival of the new regime. An estimate that 25–30% of the Hungarian economy is in the private sector may not be exaggerated;[29] the use of market mechanisms since the first significant reform in 1968 has habituated Hungarians to many aspects of the market economy. Czechoslovakia, whose communist rulers had been more rigid, started in January 1991 a series of auctions to privatize some 100,000 small businesses. There is no lack of vitality in the small business sector, particularly, so far, in Hungary and Poland. It is the larger firms in the state sector, and particularly in heavy industries such as steel and heavy chemicals, that present the main problem. These have depended on subsidies and on exports to the Soviet Union, both of which have now collapsed. This was reflected in the fall of 23% in Polish industrial production in 1990.[30] The sale of such enterprises is difficult. Many are loss-makers and, even where they are not, it is hard to value a firm in the absence of a capital market. Ministers responsible in both Hungary and Poland expect that half of industry will nevertheless be privatized before 1995.[31] Czechoslovakia and Poland, observing that orthodox methods of privatization were slow, decided to devise systems of vouchers that would distribute shares widely among the people; but Hungary, doubtful whether such a scheme would work, has preferred to continue with more normal methods of selling businesses. The rate of progress of privatization towards targets

54

such as those that the Hungarian and Polish ministers envisaged is another yardstick for the validity of reform programmes. But it is necessary also to assess whether the privatization results in viable firms and, the other side of the coin, whether firms that for the time being remain publicly owned are given the necessary autonomy to function effectively. Enterprise reform is particularly important in the financial sector, on whose efficiency all other sectors depend; and again, in establishing commercial banking, Hungary and Poland preceded Czechoslovakia.

Reform of the legal framework and enterprise system should provide the context for development of a modern physical and human structure for the economy. This will inevitably take longer. But the monitoring of progress in these respects will be another means of judging the success of the reforms – in addition, of course, to what the economy produces for the consumer, both at home and on export markets.

Economic conditions and reform in the Balkan states

Four-figure inflation in 1989 necessitated a big bang of macroeconomic policy in Yugoslavia as in Poland. The dinar was pegged in January 1990 to the deutschmark and made convertible. By the spring, with the help of a partial wage and price freeze, inflation had been eliminated. But such a freeze cannot hold without sound monetary and fiscal policies. As we saw, however, governments and banks of individual republics have undermined such policies by uncontrolled budgetary expenditure and monetary expansion. Given sound macroeconomic policies, Yugoslavia would be among the best placed of the East European countries for structural reform. Reform of the banking system is one of the keys. It has been estimated that 60% of the loans of Yugoslav banks, amounting to $10 billion, are non-performing and the prime minister, Markovic, has said that it will cost $12.5 billion to restructure the banks.[32] After macroeconomic financial and fiscal reform, such a restructuring is one of the indicators of the seriousness of Yugoslav reforms. Enterprise reform is another: some 90% of productive assets are held in a form of social ownership that neither encourages responsibility in their use nor allows for their transfer to those who would use them efficiently. There, however, individual republics can act; thus Slovenia has been privatizing firms on a substantial scale. If the Yugoslav state fails to move rapidly to a valid economic and political reform, it is likely that Slovenia and perhaps Croatia will take the law into their own hands, at least as far as economic reform is concerned. Whether it is undertaken by Yugoslavia as a whole or by separate republics, the criteria for successful reform are clear: there should be valid reform of macroeconomic policy and of the banking and enterprise systems. Beyond that, Yugoslavs do not have far to go to reach a market economy.

Bulgaria had a long experience of stability based on orthodox communist doctrine, reluctance to reform and dependence on the Soviet Union. It became starkly evident that this system was unable to meet the challenges of the contemporary international economy when Bulgaria suspended payments of principal and interest on its $10 billion external debt in March 1990. Hard currency exports were in the process of plunging by a quarter between 1989 and 1990. Then the collapse of trade in Comecon, which accounted for four-fifths of its trade, hit Bulgaria particularly hard. Inflation reached a three-figure annual rate by the end of 1990; subsidies accounted for nearly one-third of budgetary expenditure and the budget deficit rose to 10% of GDP; and total production, industrial production and gross investment all fell by 13–14% in that year. Faced with both domestic and external crises, the government announced its intention to carry out a programme of macroeconomic stabilization in 1991, together with structural reforms such as a new banking system, laws for foreign trade and investment, a privatization programme and a stock exchange.[33] Bulgaria needs PHARE assistance to help it with these reforms; but it will have to make substantial progress with them along the lines indicated earlier for the Central Europeans before it can be offered a Europe Agreement.

Romania suffers the crippling defect that the economic as well as other aspects of its civil society were grossly suppressed by the Ceausescu regime. Against this, it is relatively small consolation that the external debt was paid off. The economy was already declining in Ceausescu's last year. In 1990, net material production fell by one-tenth, industrial production by one-fifth, and gross investment by one-third. Given the failure of a coherent opposition to the former communists to emerge, it is not so surprising that Romania has made less progress than Bulgaria in preparing programmes for reform. While Romania has qualified for PHARE aid, it is even further than Bulgaria from meeting the criteria of an associate with the Europe Agreement. For Albania the distance is yet greater.

Economic conditions and reform in the Soviet Union

After seven decades with scant experience of a market economy, the prospects of transition to it are more problematic and harder to evaluate for the Soviet Union than for the Central Europeans.[34] The industrial culture of a command economy has become more deeply entrenched. People are more suspicious of private enterprise, income differentials and the price mechanism. International competition is a more remote concept. Such attitudes are both product and cause of an ossified system. Growth, which had been fast in the 1950s, slowed steadily until it appears virtually to have ceased since the mid-1980s, when investment reached as much as a quarter of GDP, while contributing little or nothing to growth.[35] By 1990, official statistics recorded a fall in total output of 4%. By the first quarter of 1991, it was 12% less than the year before; and central planners were expecting it to fall by 11.6%, and maybe as much as 16%, for the year as a whole.[36] The old system of command-administrative economy had ceased to work and was not being replaced through a coherent process of reform. Reformers had been divided between those who propounded a step-wise approach that was limited, particularly with respect to property ownership, by what conservative leninists would tolerate, and those who wanted a big bang of structural reform but understandably, given the lack of experience of changing such a deeply-entrenched system, lacked a sufficiently convincing pro-gramme to achieve it. No significant steps were taken until the with-drawal of large-denomination rouble notes and the price rises early in 1991, neither of which measures was carried out in such a way as to engender confidence in the results.

The result was a crisis that raised fear of a frightening slide into penury and disruption. The political conflict between conservatives and reformers and between centre and republics impeded not only economic reform, but also economic managers' efforts at good housekeeping. In the first quarter of 1991, republics withheld three-quarters of the tax they were due to pass to the centre, thus running the central budget into a deficit of roubles 31 billion for the quarter, more than the already excessive deficit planned for the year as a whole. In the absence of a capital market, such deficits can be covered only by printing money, hence by inflation.

Economic disruption contributed to a fall in oil production that sharply cut the predominant source of hard currency earnings. Net debt had risen by the end of 1990 to $55 billion, with servicing of some $11 billion due in 1991 on top of $5 billion to cut the backlog of trade debts. The report by the IMF, World Bank, OECD and BERD considered an estimate of a hard currency deficit of $11 billion for 1991, based on an oil price of $20 a barrel and export volume down by a quarter, to be a pessimistic one; yet the outcome could well be worse. Without western support, there would have to be import cuts deep enough to cause yet more severe disruption.

The Soviet government will doubtless continue to aim for reforms, with measures to move towards internal convertibility, to attract foreign investment, to reduce the fiscal deficit, to privatize small businesses and to allow for privatization of agriculture, although it has remained reluctant to grasp the nettle of general reform of the enterprise system.[37] But structural reforms can hardly succeed without macroeconomic stabilization; and both depend on a resolution of the conflict between centre and republics, most particularly the Russian republic. Stabilization depends on the centre obtaining its share of tax; the largest foreign investment projects, in oil and other national resources, depend on clarity as to whether centre or republics have sovereignty over them. Much else depends on a peace settlement in this 'war of laws'. A first condition for the success of economic reform is, then, resolution of the conflict between centre and republics. A second is macroeconomic stabilization. Only then can judgment about the prospects for structural reform, as discussed above with respect to the Central Europeans, become relevant; and such judgments will depend on the outcome of the struggle between reformers and conservatives. In the spring of 1991, optimism does not come easily. But it would be unwise to ignore the resilience and the ability to muddle through that the Russian people have displayed at critical junctures in their history.

5

CENTRAL EUROPEANS AND EUROPE AGREEMENTS

By the start of 1991, the European Community had responded vigorously to the reforms in Eastern Europe. Its protection against imports from the area had been greatly reduced. The Community, together with its member states, had allocated ecu 4.1 billion of grants and ecu 7.0 billion of loans. The Commission was coordinating the PHARE programme of aid from the G24 group of advanced industrial countries. But these responses had inevitably been ad hoc. The need was seen to put the relationship between the Community and East Europeans on a more secure and coherent footing.

In August 1990, following the approval by the European Council in June of Britain's suggestion that East European countries be associated with the Community, the Commission sent its communication to the Council and the European Parliament, containing its ideas for a form of association, to be called Europe Agreements, with countries of Eastern Europe.[1] They were to be for those countries giving practical evidence of the commitment to economic and political reforms: economic liberalization in order to create market economies; politically, the rule of law, human rights, multi-party systems and fair elections. Finding that Czechoslovakia, Hungary and Poland had provided such evidence, the Commission proposed that talks with them should begin. Reforms in Yugoslavia, the Commission observed, had not yet reached that point; Bulgaria and Romania were further down the line. In September, the Council gave its general approval to these ideas and in December it authorized the Commission to open negotiations with the three Central European countries.[2] Negotiations began at once with the intention that the Agreements should enter into force on 1 January 1992.[3]

Given the similarity of aims, the Agreements with each country require similar structures. But since the circumstances of the countries to be associated differ significantly, the Agreements have to be tailor-made to each.

Aims

Stable democracies and market economies in Central Europe could, as suggested in Chapter 1, make a significant contribution to the security of the Community and to the dynamism of the European economy. A primary aim of the Europe Agreements must therefore be to help the Central Europeans to succeed with their economic and political reforms. This will not be done in a year or two: it will be the better part of a decade before the economies will be internationally competitive without special measures of protection, and some time before we can be sure that democracy has really taken root. Until both conditions have been securely established, the consolidation of the reforms should take precedence over short-term commercial advantage for the existing member states.

As the reforms succeed, association will nevertheless bring considerable economic advantage to the Community as well as to the Associates. The second major aim of the Agreements should therefore be to strengthen EC-Associate relations, so that such advantage can be maximized. The immediate candidates for association, Czechoslovakia, Hungary and Poland, have all made explicit their intentions that the Agreements should lead to membership.[4] The Community, for its part, was wary of commitment. The Commission went so far as to state that the possibility of accession 'would not be affected by the conclusion of association agreements'.[5] De facto this is simply not the case. The conclusion of the Agreements will lead to changes in laws, policies and the real economies that will greatly facilitate future accessions. We will return to the question of the relationship between the Europe Agreements and future membership.

Industrial free trade

Past association agreements have provided for free trade in industrial products between the Community and the Associate, and the Europe Agreements are to do the same. Tariffs and quotas are to be phased out by both parties. The Community, as the stronger partner, has previously liberalized the faster; and this pattern is being repeated, with the Community moving far towards free trade in a first five-year phase, while the Associates reduce their protection more slowly, before catching up to complete the freeing of trade in a second phase that completes the transitional period inside ten years. Already in 1990, the Community had moved far towards free trade by applying the Generalized System of Preferences (GSP) and removing or suspending most of its quotas on imports of industrial products – with the important exceptions of textiles, steel and coal – from East European countries. Thus the main immediate effect of the Agreements on the Community's industrial imports will be to consolidate what has already been done and bind the Community not to restore the former protection. Since the generalized preferences are not contractual but are accorded by unilateral decision, this will detach these intra-European tariff arrangements from the GSP, which is intended for third world countries, and thus remove a source of some embarrassment.[6]

One of the principal benefits of association is that it provides a stable framework for the development of trade and for investment to take advantage of the trading opportunities. The risk that tariffs and quotas might be reimposed would deter some of the initiatives required for such trade and investment. The binding of the Community's liberalization is therefore significant, even if the provisions of the Agreement would no longer bind the Community were the Associate to abandon its commitment to democracy or to the market economy. That is not to say that the Community would automatically sever its liberalization. When Greece and Turkey, as Associates, lapsed from democratic government, the Community, expecting that the lapses would be temporary, suspended some aspects of the Agreements but continued with others. Nevertheless, the Community should be free to determine its policy in such circumstances, with the aim of contributing to the restoration of the reforms if possible, but with the right to revert to a different form of relationship if not.

Beyond the liberalization already achieved, Agreements include a timetable for the progressive removal of the Community's tariffs and quotas. Hungary proposed that the Community remove its tariffs in three years from the starting date, although the Community preferred the more normal period of five years.[7] A further impediment to trade has been the Community's practice of applying separate quotas to imports into each member state, in order to distribute the burden of adjustment. This is incompatible with the completion of the single market and should in any case come to an end before 1993. The removal of quotas on textiles is being negotiated separately under the renewal of MFAs as part of the Uruguay round. But this should not preclude a faster liberalization in relation to the Associates, provided that they remove their subsidization of this sector. The Community agreed, despite Greek and Portuguese opposition, to eliminate its textile tariffs by the end of the transitional period. It also overruled Spain in accepting that its protection against the Associates' steel exports would be removed during the first five-year phase.

With quotas as well as tariffs being phased out, the Community will nevertheless not be denuded of protective instruments, since it can still have recourse to anti-dumping duties and to safeguards. The Central Europeans have hitherto been on a list of state-trading countries, for which the Community, like other Gatt members, has applied a special anti-dumping regime. Since pricing in those countries lacked market rationality, judgments in cases of alleged dumping from them have been based not on an attempt to evaluate the domestic price of a product, but on criteria that neglected their comparative advantage. As market principles come to prevail, and as subsidization of enterprises ceases to be a general distortion, the state-trading list will no longer be appropriate for the Associates, and the normal anti-dumping procedures must apply. In the second phase, as the economies grow closer together, it might be useful to introduce the anti-dumping device of article 91.2 EEC, which required a member state exporting to another member state to reimport free of any restriction, thus neatly providing a sanction without recourse to time-consuming anti-dumping procedures.

Safeguards, or the Voluntary Restraint Arrangements that are associated with their potential use, are a penalty for successful exporters and can inhibit energetic exporting. Thus they undermine the purpose of the Agreements; and they should cease to be available by the end of the transitional period.

Trade is also restricted by strategic export controls. Since these apply particularly to new technologies, and in key sectors such as telecommunications, they stand in the way of industrial development. There is a clear case to retain them for exports that could contribute to the military capacity of a state that could become hostile to the Community. That could still, under some scenarios, be the case for the USSR; and the recent moves to relax the controls under CoCom are considered later in the section on the Soviet Union. Meanwhile, there have been negotiations with Central Europeans on how they can provide an adequate guarantee against onward transmission of sensitive products or technologies until such time as no further danger may be perceived from potentially adversary powers. Although these negotiations are separate from those for the Europe Agreements, the arrangements for association will remain incomplete until they are successfully concluded. The Community as such has an interest in them; and for this reason, as well as for the completion of the single market, it may be desirable, in the context of the Intergovernmental Conference on political union, to amend article 223 EEC, which has enabled member states to keep arms trade, and hence CoCom, out of the sphere of Community competence.

The Commission's Communication on the Europe Agreements also referred to 'measures having equivalent effect' to quantitative restrictions on imports, echoing the words used in article 30 EEC to describe many of the non-tariff distortions to trade that are the subject of the programme to complete the single market by the end of 1992. This is also the subject of the negotiations between the EC and Efta to establish a European Economic Area (EEA). If these negotiations succeed, similar methods could be employed under the Europe Agreements as with the Efta countries. Any difficulties are not likely to concern the substance of the *acquis* of Community laws that compose the framework of the single market. The Eftans have accepted this with few exceptions, and the Central Europeans, starting with a *tabula rasa* of such legislation, have already shown themselves ready to follow the Community pattern. The Central Europeans do, however, face a formidable task in enacting and applying the great volume of necessary laws while lacking many of the necessary administrative and legal skills; and for this they need time and much technical assistance from the Community. But the basic problem of principle, which has caused difficulty in the EC-Efta negotiations, has been to reconcile a group of states that have agreed to exercise the rule of law in the way the Community has done – that is through common political institutions enacting laws, and common juridical institutions applying them direct to firms and citizens as well as to member states and Community institutions – with states that have not accepted such a legal order.[8]

The difficulty with regard to the enactment of laws is to enable the states outside the Community to have some influence over the legislative process without making it more unwieldy than it already is and without diluting the significant democratic control that the European Parliament exerts over single-market legislation. For standards and norms, it has been possible for the EC and Efta to compose some joint mandates to the European standards institutions, which include representatives from Efta countries, to draw up common European standards. But if Eftans or Central Europeans want more influence over legislation than the Community, including the Parliament, without whose assent these agreements cannot be enacted, is prepared to tolerate, then a single market cannot be completed for the EEA.

The application of laws, once they are accepted, presents still trickier problems. The Community enables legal persons to secure their rights under Community law through the Community courts. If there is an illegal non-tariff distortion, an enterprise whose trade is damaged by it can thus secure its removal. Associates will have to satisfy the Community that they can assure the same rights to Community enterprises; and, given the rather wide scope for interpretations by the Court of Justice in its judgments on the compatibility of the mutual recognition of standards with the protection of consumers, health, safety and the environment, the procedure of mutual recognition is far from offering Associates an easy way to ensure reciprocal treatment in their legal systems. Nor is it only a matter of the courts. The EC Commission performs in the Community essential functions in controlling state aids and cartels or monopolies that distort competition; and in an EEA the Community must be satisfied that it will be similarly protected from damage by subsidies or anti-competitive practices in the other participants. It is to be hoped that, with the help of the thinking that has gone into the EEA negotiation, it will be possible to devise for the Associates arrangements that will carry conviction that Central Europe will be part of the single market by the end of the transitional period, for this is an important element in encouraging investment of foreign capital on a scale that will bring real dynamism to the Associates' economies. The expectation of eventual membership would, of course, be the most confidence-building element of all.

Agriculture

Farm products have comprised about a quarter of the exports from Eastern Europe to the Community. Only for Czechoslovakia has the proportion been a small one. Without the heavy protection of Community agriculture, this trade would have been considerably bigger. With farms in the eastern countries made more efficient by a market system, the potential could be greatly increased.[9] Already in 1990, Polish agriculture responded to the new conditions and began to export again, following the failures that led to the need for food aid in the previous winter. The Hungarians and Poles have a strong interest in better access to the Community market for their farm produce. The Community has granted some concessions already, but mostly for minor items, such as geese, mushrooms and soft fruit, although the access granted for lamb has been more significant. Poland has had a substantial quota on an annual basis for the sale of beef in the Community market with the levy reduced by 70%, while Hungary and Romania have benefited to the extent of 60%. The Hungarians and Poles are looking for much more than this, particularly for the major products, such as cereals, beef, lamb and dairy products, whereas the Community is more inclined to improve access, despite Spanish reluctance, for less salient items, such as fruit, vegetables, pork and game.

Central Europeans are not likely to forget that the Community gave East Germany access for its agricultural products free of levies and of tariffs through the long years of the command economy there. In the Europe Agreements, the Community falls far short of that, although preferential access for their agricultural exports would be the most efficient means of enabling the Hungarians and Poles to earn more hard currency in the short term. But, over the medium to longer term, the best hope is not for trade diversion from overseas suppliers to the Central Europeans, but trade creation that follows from a radical reform of Community agricultural policy, leading to lower prices and production. The pressures for this from the budget and the Gatt are already strong. By the spring of 1991 the Commission was proposing radical reform of the common agricultural policy in order to deal with mounting surpluses and expenditure; and in addition to the demands of the Uruguay round, it was becoming clear that the US would be insistent that the Community, in concluding the Europe Agreements, should respect article XXIV of the Gatt, which requires free trade areas to liberalize 'substantially all' of trade, implying the removal of much of the restriction of trade in agricultural products. The economic and political logic of allowing the Community's eastern neighbours to exercise their comparative advantage in agriculture, to the benefit of both the Community's consumers and the eastern economies, adds considerable weight to the case for reform. Nor is it seemly for the Community to insist that eastern countries abandon price controls and a system of import levies and export subsidies which have insulated their industries from international market forces, while at the same time insisting that it retain just such a system for its own agriculture.

Services and capital

East–West trade in services has hitherto been very limited, with exceptions in tourism and transport,[10] because the low regard in which the service sector was held by communists led them to inhibit the growth of an export capability and to show little interest in imports. The Community is strong in much of the sector and has an interest in the opening of the eastern markets for services. The freeing of this trade is analogous to the alignment of regulations relating to trade in goods, while the alternative of 'home-country treatment', which places the firms of partner countries offering services on the same footing as domestic firms, is analogous to the principle of mutual recognition. Since the Central Europeans are at present weak in most of the sector, although with medium-term potential as a result of their low salaries and fairly high educational standards, they may wish to maintain protection for it until they have become stronger – although it would seem to be in their interests that financial and other services for business be developed as rapidly as possible, and hence with a major contribution from western firms.

For the integration of financial markets and freeing of capital movements, too, the Community with its powerful financial institutions is the demander. It has completely freed the movement of capital among most member states; and since some of them have no controls on the movement of capital to other destinations, attempts by others to control outward movements can hardly be effective for long. So providing in the Europe Agreements for the free flow of capital to the Associates costs the Community nothing. Given their need for foreign investment and for an effective capital market, this flow is of no small importance to them.

The Associates, for their part, will wish to keep their capital at home while they are developing their capital markets and the habit of investing in their own economies. With a free flow of capital abroad, many investors would choose the safer prospect of placing their money in the advanced industrial countries, thus leaving investment in Central Europe to the foreigner, and risking either an inadequate supply of capital, or a nationalist backlash, or both. The Associates are justified in withholding reciprocity in freedom of movement for capital, apart from the capital required to finance the trade in goods and services, until they have generated a satisfactory flow of savings into a properly functioning capital market; and this will be some years ahead. The priority has rightly been seen as favourable treatment of foreign investors, including the right to repatriate profits. The Community can hasten the day when the Associates free the movement of their own capital by giving assistance in the creation of the necessary financial institutions and of incentives to encourage savings. As the institutions and the savings become more adequate, the Associates' capital markets should begin to link in with the international capital market; and there should then be progress towards freedom of capital exports and the integration of financial markets during the second phase of the transitional period.

Convertibility is, on the contrary, more urgent if trade and foreign investment are to play their due parts in regenerating the economies. Poland, in 1990, helped by a $1 billion stand-by facility, made the zloty convertible for all legal transactions undertaken by residents, with Czechoslovakia following in 1991 and Hungary due to do so in 1992. Any Associates that do not retain or achieve such convertibility, with a single exchange rate calculated to secure equilibrium in the balance of payments, should be constrained by a timetable for doing so. Beyond that, it is desirable for the success of the agreements to avoid exchange-rate instability.[11] The Poles pegged the zloty to the dollar, though in May 1991 they introduced a flexible rate measured against a trade-weighted currency basket; and the Yugoslavs pegged the dinar to the mark. The ecu, as the basket of currencies of member states of the Community, which will be the Associates' principal trading partner, appears more suitable, and the Community could encourage them to peg their currencies to it. Later, this could develop into attachment to the exchange-rate mechanism, in preparation for the Associates' participation in economic and monetary union on their becoming members of the Community.

Arguments have been advanced for and against an East European Payments Union,[12] analogous to the (in effect West) European Payments Union that went along with Marshall Aid and served as an antechamber for Europeans before they were ready to enter the international monetary system as full partners. Central Europeans have pre-empted the issue by going direct for international convertibility, which has the great merits of lending credibility to their macroeconomic policies and of linking them firmly to the world price system. But the idea of an East European Payments Union could be kept in reserve in case their first efforts at convertibility should fail or other eastern countries should wish to pursue it.

Movement of people

The Community's fourth freedom, along with free movement of goods, services and capital, is freedom of movement for people. The Poles proposed that their Europe Agreement should provide for complete freedom of movement for people between Poland and the Community by the end of the transitional period, i.e. within a decade. Meanwhile, they wanted rapid progress in liberalization, treatment no less favourable than other non-member states, and legal status for Polish migrants who may already be working in the Community without it. Without such measures, they suggested, the number of Poles working illegally in the Community is likely to increase. Hungary, with less pressure from Hungarians to work in the Community, proposed that the Community accept that a modest quota of work permits be issued for skilled Hungarians to work there for limited periods. This would help to upgrade the skills of their workforce and would offer a basis from which to expand should labour shortage induce the Community to adopt a more liberal policy in a few years' time.

The Community entered the negotiations with a restrictive posture. The Council allowed the Commission to offer little more than improvements in working conditions and social security for workers already legally established there. The Community feels under growing pressure with respect to migration. The number and status of Turkish workers in Germany have been among the vexed questions relating to the Turkish association with the Community. In 1990 West Germany, where many Central Europeans would like to work, received nearly a million Germans from elsewhere. The flow from East to West Germany will certainly continue; and there are another 3 million people of German origin, 2 million in the USSR and the rest mostly in Poland and Romania, among whom many would like to follow those who have already moved. The Poles themselves are expecting many of the million or so Polish people living in the Soviet Union to emigrate to Poland; and the flow from the 2 million Hungarians in Romania could become a flood. Such migration into Central Europe could have a knock-on effect in pressure to work in the Community; and estimates of the number of Soviet citizens who would wish to work in the West have varied between 3 million and 6 million.[13]

Although governments fear the effect of migrant workers from the East on increasingly xenophobic populations, there are strong arguments for the Community to be more liberal in relation to the Central European Associates. There are grounds to fear the impact of high unemployment on their political stability; and the migrant workers would not only help their economies with remittances but would also demonstrate the Community's practical concern about the unemployment problem, as against disillusion that could result from resistance to the presence of Central Europeans within the Community. For peoples who have long been prevented from having the close relationships with those of other European countries that have become normal in the West, opportunities to work in the Community would also contribute to 'integration at the level of populations', which in turn would underpin the political conditions of economic integration.[14]

Without a significant programme for inward migration, the Community might expose the Europe Agreements to some risk. In so far as the member governments lack the courage for this, they could limit the damage by increasing the aid to provide social security and training for the unemployed and to expand employment by promoting job-creating investments.

Completing the Europe Agreements

Most of the hard questions arise over the 'four freedoms' of movement. The rate of removal of the Community's protection against coal, steel, textiles and agricultural products is crucial, most of all for Poland, for which they comprise over half the total value of exports to the Community. There is, however, little difficulty under the heading of cooperation, since the main function of this part of the agreements is to state the uncontroversial intention to cooperate. There are about a score of subjects for cooperation under the Europe Agreements. These resemble those listed in the trade and cooperation agreements, each of which contained a selection of subjects of particular interest in the given case. But the Europe Agreements are to be more detailed and comprehensive.

Some of the subjects concern cooperation with respect to micro-economic policies: industrial standards, certification and testing, of particular significance in the Associates' approach to the single market; scientific research and technological development, in which the Associates may be able to participate in some of the Community's programmes; and investment promotion and protection, vital for the encouragement of inward investment into the Associates. Then there are public services, such as health and safety, statistics, customs and excise, education and vocational training. Some key sectors of the economy are listed: agriculture and related industries; energy; transport; telecommunications; tourism. The environment is also important. Finally, cooperation is proposed in culture, among economists, and in finance.

This last is crucial. Cooperation is not likely to amount to much unless there is money to pay for it; and, for some time ahead, most of the money will have to come from the Community. It is not surprising that the list of subjects for cooperation includes many of those in the Community's PHARE aid programmes for the East Europeans. This raises the question of how the PHARE aid is to relate to the Europe Agreements. The Community's agreements with Mediterranean countries have been accompanied by financial protocols committing it to provide given sums for each country. It has offered renewed financial protocols for the period 1991–6 to Algeria, Egypt, Israel, Jordan, Lebanon, Morocco, Syria and Tunisia, allocating a total of ecus 1.3 billion in loans and ecu 775 million in grants in specified sums for each, and at the same time a lump sum of over ecu 2 billion for the support of reforms and for 'horizontal cooperation' on subjects such as the environment and technical assistance.[15] The principal aim of the Community's aid to Eastern Europe is to support the reforms; and there are grounds for keeping this aid separate from the individual Europe Agreements, with the flexibility to allocate it among the several countries in the light of their evolving circumstances. But this does not preclude a mixed solution, as for the Mediterranean countries, with some money committed in financial protocols and the rest in a general fund – or in a collective protocol.

The working of each Europe Agreement is to be supervised by an Association Council, at the level of Ministers and Commissioners, able to take decisions by mutual agreement and to discuss wider international questions. The Council's work is to be prepared by an Association Committee of senior officials, who will be able to 'ensure continuity' between meetings of the Council. There is also to be a Parliamentary Association Committee, in which members of parliament from each Associate will meet members of the European Parliament for discussions, and which can make recommendations to the Association Council. Disputes are to be settled within these institutions if possible; otherwise they can go to arbitration, as is already the case in the agreement with Yugoslavia. The right of the Association Councils to discuss wider questions beyond the working of the agreements opens the way to general political dialogue, which the Associates regard as important.

Beyond the formal institutions, cooperation under the agreements can foster a network of less formal relationships, between, for example, political parties in the Community and those of the Associates and between all kinds of unofficial and official bodies;[16] and this will be a matter for aid and cooperation.

The Europe Agreements are to be of indefinite duration, although their operation must depend on the successful transition of the Associates to pluralist democracy and market economy. The transitional period, within the Gatt norm of up to ten years, is designed to give time for the necessary adjustments, with the Community removing most of its barriers in the first phase, while the Associates prepare themselves for the second phase in which they are to complete most of their liberalization. The Community made clear its intention to ensure, before embarking on the second phase, that the Associate had made enough progress in establishing a market economy as well as consolidating its democracy. The Hungarians in particular resisted providing in the Agreements for a formal review of such progress. But the Agreements are anyway to allow for renunciation by either side if the conditions on which they are based are not met. If the reforms were to be reversed, the Agreements could not be regarded as irreversible; nor should the Community be obliged to remove all measures of protection if an Associate fails to conduct its trade according to normal market principles.

Since the Agreements are intended to enter into force on 1 January 1992, the timetable is tight. After completion of the negotiations, the Community's Council has to enact them by unanimity and, because article 238 EEC was amended by the Single European Act, the European Parliament has to give its assent. Nor is that all. These are 'mixed agreements' in that they contain articles on subjects, such as cultural cooperation and political dialogue, that are dealt with, not under Community competence, but under that of the member states, which will therefore also have to ratify them. This process will be time-consuming and it may be that, if the major parts of the Agreements that come under Community competence are to enter into force on time, a formula will have to be found for delaying the formal application of the remainder until the member states have all ratified.

Among the hard choices with which the negotiations have confronted the Community, agriculture and migration have been mentioned. The question of eventual membership for the Associates was another contentious point. The Associates asked for this prospect to be written into the Europe Agreements, following the examples of the Greek association agreement, which foresaw ultimate Greek membership both in the preamble and in its article 72, and of the Turkish one, which also referred to it in the preamble and, somewhat less confidently, in article 24 to the effect that the two parties could consider the possibility if and when the conditions for it had been met. The Community has doubtless been embarrassed by the purchase this afforded to Turkish diplomacy, for there is no such mention at all in the association agreements for Cyprus and for Malta. Yet there were strong arguments for referring in the Europe Agreements to the possibility of eventual membership.

The completion of the Europe Agreements themselves will anyway

71

depend on fulfilment by the Associates of the conditions of pluralist democracy and market economy, which would be the principal conditions for membership. If these conditions have been met at the end of the transitional period of the Europe Agreement but an Associate is still not seen to be sufficiently competitive or presents other difficult problems, then a transitional period of membership can be provided, as has been done for all new members of the Community hitherto. Some in the Community may fear the entry of Central European countries for protectionist reasons, just as Spanish accession was delayed by opposition from farmers in France and Italy who did not want to face Spanish competition. Others may be concerned that the Community's institutions would become unworkable with the growing membership. But too much is at stake in the new Central European democracies for such considerations to stand in the way of their eventual accession. The protectionists will have to be overruled as they were in the Iberian case; and the institutions will have to be strengthened so that they can cope with the new members. If the Central Europeans' aspirations for membership were to be rebuffed, the prospects for their western orientation and for their democratic progress could be damaged, whereas the more likely their eventual membership seems to be, the more confidently foreign firms will invest in them.[17] *The Financial Times* has good grounds for its view that the aim of membership for Czechoslovakia, Hungary and Poland by the year 2000 'should be an imperative'.[18] The Community was right to accept that membership could be recognized as an objective in the preamble to the Europe Agreements; and the Agreements should be seen as the principal element in a strategy to bring it about.

6
POLICIES TOWARDS THE SOVIET UNION AND THE BALKAN STATES

The relationship with the Soviet Union, as a great power, is of a different order of importance for the Community and its member states from that with the East Europeans. The Community does not therefore regard a Europe Agreement as suitable for the Soviet Union, but has been considering other arrangements to which we will return later in the chapter. The offer of association is, however, open in principle to all East European countries, although the Balkan states are less ripe for it than the Central Europeans and differ widely among themselves.

BALKAN STATES

Yugoslavia has long had a closer relationship with the Community than have the other East European countries. The liberalization that the Community granted to Hungary and Poland and then extended to other East Europeans in 1990 did not add much to what Yugoslavia already had; the Community was, indeed, bound by agreement to maintain the Yugoslavs' right to free entry, while conceding the others their privileges unilaterally. Yugoslavia's only substantial gain from the Community's new eastern policy was ecu 35 million, which it was allocated in 1990 under the PHARE programme, much less than that to Hungary and Poland but useful all the same.

Nor would a Europe Agreement effect much change in the short term in Yugoslavia's trading arrangements with the Community. Some small adjustments would follow for tariffs and quotas on Community imports of industrial products. Not much more would be expected for agriculture. Yugoslavia would be required to reciprocate the liberalization over the medium term. This might be seen by some as a deterrent; but Yugoslav policy-makers became decreasingly protectionist in recent years. Over the longer term, a Europe Agreement should improve the prospects for participation in the single market and for agricultural exports; and it could promptly lead to a larger share of aid from the Community. It would ensure that Yugoslavia was on the inside track with respect to any new developments; and it would improve the prospect for eventual accession. Although most such benefits may be for the medium or longer term, the response on the part of foreign investors could be much quicker, as they gained confidence in the future of the Yugoslav economy. So Yugoslavia has good grounds for its stated wish for a Europe Agreement.

The Commission, in its Communication on the Europe Agreements, wrote that the Community would take the long-standing relations with Yugoslavia into account in 'determining the calendar for exploratory talks with Yugoslavia', but would also have to take account of 'the fulfilment of commitments to reform'. In December 1990, the EC–Yugoslav Cooperation Council, meeting in the context of the trade and cooperation agreement, expressed in its joint declaration the wish that reforms would be pursued towards pluralist democracy and market economy, and its confidence that the continuation of this process would enable the conditions of association to be fulfilled.[1] Behind these formulations was the concern that, without crucial measures of political reform, the creation of the conditions for association would remain blocked, despite the distance that Yugoslavia has travelled over the years in the direction of a market economy.

Having broken with the stalinist model in the early 1950s when the self-management enterprise system was introduced, and having initiated a wide range of market mechanisms from 1965 onwards, Yugoslavia's need for reform is focused on the financial and enterprise systems. Banking reform is needed in order to prevent the banks from undermining microeconomic efficiency by non-performing loans that are in fact subsidies to enterprises, and from undermining macroeconomic policy by uncontrolled credit expansion. An effective capital market requires a rational measure of the value of enterprises, which the present ownership system does not provide. The central bank does not have control over the supply of money and credit in the economy. Prime Minister Markovic has shown that he seriously intends to effect the necessary financial reforms. But the political system has not enabled him to carry out his intentions.

Political reform has also gone far. On top of the long-standing latitude for civil society, multi-party elections were conducted in the constituent republics in 1990. But crucial elements of pluralist democracy are not complete. An insufficiently reformed communist party still controls Serbia, the dominant republic; and Markovic's reformist government is unable to make its policies effective in the absence of a workable relationship between the centre and the republics. Early in 1990, with the programme for economic reforms and for elections, the Community was on the point of starting negotiations for association. But the difficulties with both economic and political reform caused it to draw back; and the crisis in relations between Serbia and other republics, in particular Slovenia and Croatia, and between the republics and the centre, may present the Community with some very difficult decisions.

Although the EC–Yugoslav Cooperation Council expressed the hope that reforms would make Yugoslav association possible, the Community may equally be faced by an insufficiently reformed central government system, and by one or more republics that wish themselves to negotiate Europe Agreements. This would be fairly readily manageable if the republics had separated constitutionally from the Yugoslav state or if that state had been converted into a confederal system, with the republics holding the powers required to negotiate association.[2] The Community already works with the republics, even if this is done through the central government. The prime minister of Slovenia, meeting Commissioner Abel Matutes in February 1991 with the Yugoslav ambassador present, said that Slovenia wanted more autonomy for the republics and closer relations with the Community. At a press conference afterwards, however, he said that Slovenia wanted, in time, to join the Community.[3]

The Community has expressed its preference for 'preservation of the unity and territorial integrity of Yugoslavia', first in the concluding statement from the European Council of 27–28 October 1990, and again, in the same words, in the joint declaration of the Cooperation Council. But the Community has also expressed its support for human rights in Yugoslavia and for the reforms. If unity and democracy should prove incompatible in Yugoslavia, because of repression directed against the republics that have credible reform programmes, the Community may have to choose between supporting Yugoslav unity or supporting democracy and human rights. If repressive force is used to constrain one or more democratic republics, the Community should act decisively to support the democrats. The economic instruments at the Community's disposal could be powerful, when account is taken of giving or withholding aid as well as sticks or carrots for trade. But it cannot be excluded that the Community should go beyond the use of economic instruments, through the procedures of European Political Cooperation or elsewhere. Here again, the Community may find itself in urgent need of a greater capacity for the formation and conduct of a common foreign policy, and maybe security policy too. Germany and Italy have carried the most weight in forming Community policy in relation to Yugoslavia, with Greece also having a particular interest. This may, in view of the potential dangers, be an area in which Britain should seek a more important role, encouraging contingency planning on the part of the Community as well as reacting to events.

Meanwhile, negotiations for the future trade regime between Yugoslavia and the Community are to begin, under the trade and cooperation agreement, in 1991; and the Cooperation Council expressed the hope that this could be done in the perspective of an association agreement, with the aim of establishing a free trade area. Given the necessary reforms, this should be a feasible aim for the end of this decade. At the same time a new financial protocol is to be negotiated, dealing again with transport infrastructure; and Yugoslavia will, short of violent mishaps, continue to benefit from aid under the PHARE programme.

The governments of Bulgaria and Romania, too, have expressed their desire for association with the Community. The Commission, for its part, had expressed the view that it would be necessary to 'monitor closely' their reforms, so that negotiations could begin 'as soon as the necessary conditions have been established'.[4] This cautious wording reflected the judgment that these two countries have further to go than Yugoslavia before their reforms could be regarded as complete, and also perhaps that their history and political experience make it harder for them to cover the distance.

Bulgaria has nevertheless taken some significant steps. Although many of the old party functionaries remain in place, including a majority in parliament capable of blocking reform legislation, the coalition government with its non-party prime minister has been developing a serious economic reform programme. If it appears likely that economic and political reforms will lead to market economy and pluralist democracy, the Community's policy indicates that negotiations for association will begin. Doubts will remain, however, whether Bulgaria could be a candidate for membership in the same time-scale as the Central Europeans. Meanwhile, Bulgaria can derive some benefits from its trade and cooperation agreement with the Community, and much from the PHARE programme and the unilateral concessions of GSP and quota liberalization. These concessions are related to the reform process. If the reforms continue successfully, the concessions can be consolidated and the aid increased until such time as Bulgaria moves forward to association. If on the other hand there were to be serious backsliding, the Community would have to consider how far the benefits should remain intact.

The repression by Romania's post-Ceausescu regime caused the Community to suspend its help for Romania until January 1991, when it placed Romania on the same footing as Bulgaria. It is to be hoped that political and economic reforms will be pursued so that the relationship between the Community and Romania can bear sufficient fruit. But a great deal more change is required before it would be appropriate to go beyond the PHARE programme and the trade and cooperation agreement and negotiate with Romania for association.

Reform in Albania is yet more problematic. But if, following the elections of March 1991, conditions improve enough to justify a trade and cooperation agreement, then the Community's policy of monitoring reforms to determine whether the time may become ripe for association should apply to Albania too. Here, as in the other countries where reforms face much difficulty, the Community will need to sharpen its capacity to evaluate the prospects for progress towards market economies and pluralist democracies.

THE SOVIET UNION

By 1990, the West was poised to give help on a large scale for the process of reform in the Soviet Union. Following the remarkable growth of free expression and the new democratic elements in political institutions, hopes grew that there would be radical economic reform to introduce a market economy. It was at the same time clear that vast economic problems would have to be overcome if reform was to succeed. By the middle of the year, there was strong momentum in the West for a major effort to assist. Germany, in the process of securing its unification, in the course of which the Federal Republic became committed to aid of DM 12 billion (ecu 5.7 billion) to ease the Soviet Union's removal of over a third of a million troops from the eastern Länder, gave the strongest push for a big effort on the part of the West. The Germans, together with the French, pressed their western partners to agree to offer large sums of direct cash assistance.[5] But Britain, Japan and the US were reluctant; and the compromise at the G7 summit in Houston in July was that the IMF, World Bank, OECD and BERD would together make a study of the

Soviet economy on which to base decisions by the end of the year. This was duly produced, as well as a study on the same subject that the Commission undertook on behalf of the Community and in close cooperation with those responsible for the other study.[6]

By December 1990, the Community was ready for a striking policy initiative towards the Soviet Union. The European Council of heads of state and government, meeting in Rome on 14–15 December, decided to offer the Soviet Union an agreement whose flavour is best caught by the French term for it: *un grand accord.*[7] This was evidently to be similar to an association agreement in many ways, though without the commitment to free trade. Clearly quotas would be liberalized ahead of the timetable that was fixed in the trade and cooperation agreement. It was not clear, however, what trade advantages would be offered beyond that, apart from those that might be agreed under the energy charter which the European Council also proposed and which, given the structure of Soviet exports, would cover the products that comprise the bulk of them. There would be political and cultural cooperation as well as 'economic cooperation'. The latter, as we have seen in relation to the trade and cooperation agreements, would probably not amount to much if not accompanied by financial assistance. But the European Council also decided upon a substantial programme of aid: food aid of ecu 250 million in the form of grants; credits guaranteed for food supplies up to ecu 500 million; technical assistance of ecu 400 million. The Community also decided to send a senior official to represent it in Moscow, with a small office of half a dozen people.

Since the autumn, there had been signs that the reformers were losing out to the conservatives in the Soviet regime; and in January 1991 the high hopes for reform were dashed, with the repression in the Baltic republics, the departure from government of most of the remaining reformers, and the growing power of the conservative forces. The Community reacted to the repression by suspending its food aid and technical assistance programme and by postponing a meeting of the joint committee under the trade and cooperation agreement, which had made a promising start in 1990.

It was never likely that the path of reform in the Soviet Union would be smooth, and setbacks should not cause surprise. Reforms may nevertheless continue and hence justify large-scale western help. But the events of January were a reminder that there is also the downside: that the Community needs to be ready also to react more negatively to events in the Soviet Union. It is to be hoped that sanctions will not again be necessary to respond to aggressive or repressive behaviour outside the Soviet Union's frontiers. But a reversion to that remains conceivable, given the instability in the Balkans and the Middle East, and the possibility of dissension about the troops still in the eastern part of Germany. The Community needs to be prepared for such eventualities should the regime fall into more reactionary hands.

If the Community has to face neither the unhappy outcomes of reaction or chaos, nor the welcome prospect of credible reform, but something in between, it will have to make the best of the routine of the trade and cooperation agreement, though this may be combined with some interesting developments with the energy charter and the technical assistance programme. Other business may include some further relaxation of CoCom controls and negotiation of terms for financing the Soviet Union's external deficit. The relationship with the Soviet Union is so important that such matters, with their potential for affecting the climate of relations and the chances of steps towards a market economy, must be of no small interest to the Community.

Energy

Tariffs and quotas do not touch the oil and gas that comprise the greater part of the Soviet Union's capacity to earn hard currencies, so these commodities do not enter into the Community's normal trade negotiations. But, although access to the Community market is free, the trading conditions could be improved by measures to ensure the security and stability of supplies and markets. Such is the rationale for the proposed energy charter.

It was at the European Council in Dublin in June 1990, when the heads of state and government were seeking ways to develop the relationship with the Community's eastern neighbours, that Ruud Lubbers, the Dutch prime minister, put forward his proposal for an 'energy community' to embrace all European states. His use of the word community gave some the impression that he envisaged a supranational organization. But he made it clear at the CSCE summit in Paris in November 1990 that he was not proposing new institutions; an arrangement between the governments and the EC Commission would serve.[8] A supranational agency would, indeed, present great difficulties if some of the participating states were democracies and some were not; and the growing uncertainties in the Soviet Union, where it remained unclear whether the central or the republics' authorities were responsible for policy regarding natural resources, compounded the risks of commitment to any heavy institutional structure. The Commission was therefore asked to draft a charter for an intergovernmental grouping; and the European Council, which gave the proposal its blessing, decided in December 1990 that a European conference be convened for the second half of 1991 – when the Community's presidency will be held by the Netherlands – in order to consider the Commission's draft.

Mr Lubbers hit on a field of much potential interest, both for the Community and for a number of other European countries. Foremost among these is the Soviet Union, whose production and hence export earnings have been falling and which would benefit if western technology and capital were applied to reverse that trend. For the Community, the Iraqi war has demonstrated the risks involved in Middle East oil supplies; a diversification of sources, following on expanded exports from the Soviet Union, would spread the risk and help to stabilize the price. Within the Community, there is interest on the part both of the countries with capacity to contribute technology to Soviet modernization and of those whose concern is mainly as consumers. For the East Europeans, there is an even greater need for stable prices and secure supplies.

These interests will be reflected in the scope of the charter. The Commission's draft provides for non-discrimination in access and exploitation of resources; investment protection; progressive removal of barriers to trade; common rules or mutual recognition of rules regarding health, safety, and the protection of consumers, workers and the environment; cooperation in research and development.[9] Specific agreements can be concluded within this framework; and an international secretariat is to oversee the implementation. Since the Chernobyl disaster in 1986, the environmental consideration needs no emphasis; and the significance of energy savings can be judged from the estimate that such savings in the Soviet Union could amount to as much as one-third of its total consumption, which would release vast quantities of oil and gas for export.[10] The logic of technical assistance for energy savings and environmental protection is clear. For gas and oil in particular, moreover, an adequate basis of stability and security of supplies as well as markets could justify cooperation in technology and investment for production and transport on a very large scale. The Soviet Union has nearly two-fifths of the world's known reserves of gas, the eco-friendliest of the major fuels.[11] But to get it out of the permafrost or the ice-covered sea and into the markets in Central and Western Europe could cost scores of billions of dollars. Investment in the extraction and transport of oil could likewise be enormously costly. Western capital and technology are needed if these industries are to be modernized and developed.

The Soviet Union needs the cooperation of western enterprises and capital. But the enterprises and capital need certain guarantees if they are to invest their money and skills on a large scale. Both Soviet legislation for the protection of these investments and the conditions for expatriate staff must be adequate. With the division of economic powers between the Soviet central authorities and the republics being uncertain, notably with respect to the control of natural resources, western business cannot regard such legislation as credible; and even when those responsibilities have been clearly enough defined, companies will be justified in asking governments to share some of the political risks. The principal basis for large investments must, however, be undertakings on the Soviet side to supply, and on the western side to buy, the minimum quantities of oil and gas that can justify the cost. The charter should aim to provide a framework within which, as circumstances in the Soviet Union improve, there will be the necessary confidence in such undertakings.

Trade

Since oil and gas predominate in Soviet exports, arrangements for energy are, for the short and medium term, more important for the Community's trade with the Soviet Union than for other goods. But if reforms succeed, the Soviet Union should become a large exporter of manufactures, consequently increasing its import capacity. Since such trade would be mutually beneficial, and since the creation of a market system for the Soviet economy is in the Community's interest, Community policy should aim to demonstrate the potential benefits. This implies a liberal attitude to the early removal of import quotas. If significant steps towards market economy are taken on the Soviet side, the Community could liberalize quotas promptly, as it has for the East Europeans. Should reforms become as far-reaching as in Central Europe, the Community could suspend tariffs on imports from the Soviet Union on the scale that it has done for East Europeans, for a limited period of, say, five years, in order to improve the prospects for the reforms' success. This would, as in the case of the East Europeans, have to be done in consultation with the US and other Gatt partners. Community industries would doubtless have to be assured that safeguards against surges of Soviet exports could be effective, since there would be fears that, given the size of the Soviet economy, such surges could become floods. But the achievement of a

Soviet market economy would be of such benefit to the Community as to justify the taking of risks, if a credible programme of reform is really set in train.

It has been suggested that, should reforms succeed in making Soviet agriculture efficient, a large capacity to export cheap food would result.[12] Without radical reform of its own agricultural policy, the Community would be unable to take advantage of the resulting opportunities for trade in both directions, exchanging sophisticated western manufactures for Soviet food. The mutual benefits could be great; and this too should be weighed in the scale as the Community considers its own agricultural reform – the more so since, even if the prospect of such Soviet exports is for the longer term, there would be major benefits at shorter notice in importing agricultural products from Eastern Europe.

The controls on the export of technologies that could be used for military purposes are applied by the governments, working together in CoCom, not by the Community. These controls have prevented the export of products that could be valuable for the Soviet civilian economy. In June 1990, CoCom agreed to remove the controls on 38 of the 116 categories whose export to the Soviet Union and the East European countries associated with it had previously been banned; and preparations were made to reduce the list to eight core items, including advanced tele-communications, navigation and avionics; some computers and propulsion systems; sensoring systems; and advanced materials and machine tools. The hardening of Soviet attitudes and Iraq's abuse of its military capacity occasioned a delay in these preparations early in 1991.[13] With legislation for completion of the Community's single market to be fully in place by the end of 1992, it is hard to see how member states could maintain effective export controls without joint Community action. If circumstances continue to favour the relaxation of the controls, the Community could press the Soviet Union to reciprocate by relaxing its own controls on the export of defence-related technologies.

The question of reciprocity is not in general an easy one in relation to trade negotiations with the Soviet Union. In the absence of reform to a market system, attempts by the Soviet Union to reciprocate trade liberalization by its western partners are likely, for reasons given in Chapter 2, to lack credibility; and when serious reforms are under way, the Community may be inclined to give them a fair wind by unilateral concessions. The improvement of conditions for inward investment and for joint ventures may for some time remain the best form of reciprocation for more open access to the Community's market.

A common policy towards the Soviet Union

The relationship of trade policy with more general foreign policy was demonstrated when a meeting of the joint committee under the EC–Soviet trade and cooperation agreements that was due to be held in January 1991 was cancelled by the Community following the repression in the Baltic republics; and the same applied to the aid programme, which was suspended at the same time. The Soviet Union accepted the commitment to human rights as part of the CSCE process, enshrined in the Charter of Europe signed in Paris in November 1990; and the Community showed itself determined to react against any serious reneging on that commitment. The case of the Baltic republics was the first in which the rights of groups such as the Baltic peoples were invoked; and that raises the question of the Community's relations with republics that seek independence from the Soviet Union.

There are similarities with the situation in Yugoslavia. The Community should, if such republics seek support from it, behave correctly under international law. That may impede the conclusion of trade agreements where the constitution of the state that is formally recognized, in this case the Soviet Union, does not accord the republics the necessary powers. But the provision of aid offers more scope for relations with the republics. The structure of Soviet government, with joint committees of representatives both at the centre and in the republics, below the similarly composed Federation Council, should facilitate this; and the Community has delivered emergency aid to Lithuania without passing through the Soviet central government. Yet the centre may try to prevent direct relations between the Community and the republics; and trade policy is intrinsically harder to divide between the two than is the execution of aid programmes. But, while adhering to legality, the Community should give due weight to progress towards pluralist democracy and the rule of law, in both the republics and the Soviet Union, when deciding how to develop its relations with either.

It was with high hopes for the process of reform in the Soviet Union itself that the European Council in December 1990 launched its proposal for *un grand accord*. Although the wording implied that this might resemble an association agreement in all but the, admittedly central, element of free trade, and although the European Council expressed its desire to support 'the reforms', there was no mention of pluralist democracy or market economy, a convincing commitment to which was an explicit condition for the opening of negotiations for Europe Agreements. Yet the Charter of Europe, signed in the previous month, committed the

Soviet Union not only to human rights but also specifically to pluralist democracy, representative government and market economy. Early disappointment with the Community/Soviet relationship in 1991 reflected the Soviet failure to make enough progress towards fulfilling these commitments. The European Council's initiative should be seen as the start of an evolving relationship whose aim is to encourage progress towards market economy and pluralist democracy, and which would not reach its full development until the Soviet Union should have a credible programme for achieving these conditions. Even given their full achievement, however, accession to the Community cannot be envisaged for the Soviet Union as it is possible for East Europeans; its size, or even that of the Russian republic alone, would unbalance the Community, which needs a rough equilibrium among its major member states.

Meanwhile, the relationship may be developed on the basis of the trade and cooperation agreement, with its scope enlarged as the European Council's initiative bears fruit, and of the aid programme also launched by the European Council, which is considered in the next chapter. The European Council decided that the Community should help the Soviet Union to join the international financial institutions, in particular the IMF, with which, as also with the World Bank, a special association had been proposed for the Soviet Union in 1990. The European Council also wanted the existing limit on Soviet borrowing from the BERD to be reconsidered. More generally, the Community can try to ensure that the Soviet Union, following the dwindling away of Comecon and the Warsaw Pact, does not remain isolated in so far as it does not isolate itself.

In 1990, the Soviet Union became an observer at the Gatt, to which all the East Europeans except Albania now belong; and if its market reforms proceed, it could become a contracting party. It is an observer at the Council of Europe, which Czechoslavkia and Hungary have already joined. This offers a framework for cultural cooperation, which the European Council also wanted the Community to develop bilaterally with the Soviet Union. Full membership requires, however, acceptance of the European Convention on Human Rights and of the authority of the European Court of Human Rights, which presents a problem for the Soviet Union. The Soviet Union, unlike the Central Europeans, is also likely to remain for some time ineligible to join the OECD, whose members are democracies with market economies. But the CSCE, which was designed to contain the Soviet Union, should be used as a framework in which it can cooperate with its European and North American partners as fully as is feasible; and the Community should encourage such use.

84

There should be no encouragement, however, of the illusion that the CSCE could replace the Community itself or Nato, for the Community is based on a degree of economic, juridical and political integration, and Nato of military integration, that are not realistic objectives for the wider group, even if the Community, the US and other democracies could contemplate a measure of integration with the Soviet Union if it eventually establishes and consolidates a soundly based democracy.

At the same time as the Community seeks constructive relations with the Soviet Union, it should be prepared to defend its interests in the event of less favourable developments there. Security is fundamental. The Single European Act envisaged coordination 'on the political and economic aspects of security' (art. 30 SEA), and the Community should be ready to use its economic power should the Soviet Union threaten its interests. But with a reduction in the American contribution to Europe's defence, the need is felt for a more solid 'European pillar'. It is widely agreed that this should be created by strengthening the Western European Union (WEU), though there is difference within the Community's Intergovernmental Conference on political union between the French and Germans, who want to bring WEU closer to the Community and to merge them when the WEU Treaty expires in 1998, and the British and Dutch, who want to keep the two separate. While Europeans would be ill-advised to act in ways that would undermine American commitment to European security, the Community and its member states will be better placed to safeguard their interests in relation to the Soviet Union if the security as well as the economic instruments of policy can be coordinated within the same institutions. That would make a reality of the 'European foreign policy' that was established as an objective in the Single European Act; and the capacity to pursue such a common policy in relation to the Soviet Union is particularly significant. While the Community should be capable of a policy to defend its interests against any eventual Soviet threats, we can hope that circumstances will instead allow it to use its economic power to strengthen its relations with a reforming Soviet Union and its political capacity to further a secure and peaceful order in Europe. We need a Community with the instruments and institutions to pursue an effective common foreign policy under diverse conditions: in short a Community for all seasons.

7

INVESTMENT AND AID

Inward investment is a key to the creation of competitive market economies in Eastern Europe. It is not only the most effective way of transferring technology and all kinds of management skill. It is also the soundest way to cover the deficits in savings and in the balance of payments that will accompany the transition to a path of self-sustaining growth; and it is the royal road to integration in the international economy. At the same time as estimating that the capital needs of the East European countries would at the least be not far short of ecu 100 billion a year, the Centre for Economic Policy Research expected private savings there to be very low 'for the years to come'.[1] Although the OECD, on the contrary, has held that the finance of their reconstruction will depend on strong domestic savings flows, these are not likely to be forthcoming during the early period of reform. The Bank of International Settlements has observed that there is not much prospect of even modest flows of private foreign capital at present; and it is hard to contest the Bank's view that, in the absence of sufficient private capital, official aid is essential to fill the need for external finance, to act as a catalyst for reform, and to bring along behind it the private capital from abroad.[2]

East Europeans are aware of the need to provide incentives for foreign investors, including friendly legislation and the right to repatriate profits and capital; and, for the Central Europeans, this is underpinned by the Europe Agreements. Both these and the trade and cooperation agreements commit the Community and its partners to cooperate in actions to promote investment such as exhibitions, fairs and the provision of information. But many potential investors will hold back until they are confident that the reforms are bringing an effective market economy into being, that the infrastructure is satisfactory and that there is little danger of a political relapse. Meanwhile, official aid can help to provide a basis on which private investors will be able to build.

The BERD

The Community's initiative in creating the European Bank for Reconstruction and Development (BERD) had the particular aim of using public money from the West to help develop the private sector in Eastern Europe and the Soviet Union. This initiative was taken at the meeting of the European Council in Strasbourg in December 1989, when France wanted to end its six-month term of presidency with a constructive response to the events in the East. The project quickly secured the backing of the US, Japan, other G24 countries and a number beyond that circle, as well as the East Europeans and the Soviet Union; and the statutes were agreed by May 1990. The capital amounts to ecu 10 billion, 51% of which is subscribed by the Community's member states together with the Commission and the European Investment Bank, and 13.45% by the participants that are entitled to borrow from it, that is Bulgaria, Czechoslovakia, Hungary, Poland, Romania, Yugoslavia and the Soviet Union. The aims emphasize private enterprise as well as democracy and market economy: 'to foster the transition towards open-market oriented economies and to promote private and entrepreneurial initiative in the Central and East European countries committed to and applying the principles of multi-party democracy, pluralism and market economies.' The Bank is also, uniquely among international financial institutions, required to promote in all its activities 'environmentally sound and sustainable development'. In order to ensure that it promotes the private sector, it is required to make at least 60% of the annual total of its loans and investments to private borrowers, and at least the same proportion to private borrowers in any one country in the first five years; and it can place up to 30% of its paid-up capital into equity investments. The justification for this public institution investing in the private sector is that the transition from the Soviet-type system to pluralist democracy and market economy is a public good of such significance for the Community and other subscribers to the Bank that it is well worth while to expose public money to the risks in the early period before private capital is ready to assume them in sufficient volume. The very great difficulties faced by the Soviet Union, and the exceptional importance of any prospect for successful reforms there, might have counted in favour of giving the Bank the capacity to pay the Soviet Union special attention. But the Americans in particular argued against exposure to these risks; and the Bank is limited to lending no more than the 6% Soviet share of the capital to Soviet borrowers in the first three years. The Bank has indicated that it could lend a total of some ecu 5 billion in the first five years, raising the rate of lending to over ecu 2 billion a year in the following three years.[3]

PHARE

From the decision in July 1989 to launch the PHARE programme to aid Poland and Hungary, through its extension to include Bulgaria, Czecho-slovakia, Romania and Yugoslavia, and up to January 1991, the G24 allocated for it ecu 5.7 billion of grants, as well as ecu 9.9 billion of loans and credits from governments and the Community, together with ecu 3.9 billion from the World Bank. There was in addition the ecu 8.2 billion of capital that the G24 had by then put up for the BERD and that the Bank expects to lend at a rate of about ecu 1 billion a year in the first five years, together with the IMF support, which is based largely on finance from the G24 countries.[4] By March 1991, the aid had also come to include the writing-off of somewhat over half Poland's official debt, i.e. of some ecu 14 billion.

The lion's share of the PHARE money has come from the Community institutions, together with the member states: ecu 4.1 billion, or 72% of the grants; ecu 7.0 billion, or half of the loans and credits. The US, claiming severe budgetary constraints, had allocated ecu 763 million of grants and ecu 179 million of loans; the Japanese, ecu 1.5 billion of loans and ecu 42 million of grants. The G24 are inclined to interpret the coordination of their efforts, for which the Commission has been given responsibility, as requiring the exchange of information rather than any serious attempt to place the aid within the framework of a common policy. Since the Community is the largest contributor, and the others are not inclined to be coordinated, it seems reasonable to concentrate policy-making efforts on the programme of the Community initiatives and the member states.

Of the Community's ecu 4.1 billion of grants, ecu 2.5 billion was allocated from the Community's own budget and the rest by the member states, the largest contributors being Germany with ecu 766 million (of which ecu 665 million comprised a cancellation of Polish debt in advance of the general writing-down in March 1991), Britain with ecu 230 million, Denmark and Italy ecu 202 million each, France ecu 120 million and the Netherlands ecu 41 million. About one-half of the Community's ecu 6.2 billion of loans comprised export credits allocated by the member states, as much a form of export promotion as of aid; Germany was the biggest provider of export credits (ecu 1.7 billion allocated) as well as of other loans (ecu 1.2 billion). Belgium, France, Italy and Spain also concentrated on export credits, while Britain confined itself to grants. Of the remaining half of the Community's loans, the bulk comprised loans in general support of the Central Europeans' economies: for a Stabilization Fund for Poland, a Medium-Term Loan for Hungary and Financial Assistance for Czechoslovakia, totalling ecu 3.1 billion from the G24 as a whole. Of this the Community provided five-sixths: ecu 1.2 billion from its institutions and ecu 1.4 billion from its member states (of which ecu 1 billion from Germany).

Poland was by far the largest destination for grants: one-third of the total from the Community budget together with the member states was for Poland, with proportions between only 1% and 5% for each of the other countries and 54% unallocated. Of the ecu 2.5 billion from the Community's budget, the use of 1.8 billion remained to be specified in the programmes for 1991 and 1992; and of the remainder, over nine-tenths had been allocated to five main purposes: emergency aid (food and medical supplies, ecu 288 million), agriculture (ecu 136 million), environment (ecu 83 million), training and education (ecu 78 million, compared with ecu 107 million for this from the British government's own aid programme), and banking, trade and tourism (ecu 50 million, of which ecu 35 million was for Yugoslav financial reform).

These were the sectors in which the Commission was able to find valid uses for grants in the first year or so of the PHARE programme. For the future, the Community has chosen a small number of core areas on which to focus its assistance.[5] The first of these is privatization and the restructuring of enterprises. The Commission seeks to help the process of privatizing potentially viable state enterprises and, meanwhile, the provision of a legislative and regulatory framework for their operation as independent commercial enterprises, including the demerger of some concerns that may monopolize the whole of an industrial sector. Studies financed by the Commission may also lead to the conclusion that such a concern has no future and must be liquidated. More positively, the Commission may provide financial assistance for the beneficiary countries' agencies that promote privatization or restructuring.

A second core area is the restructuring and modernization of banking and financial services. Here the Commission offers assistance for advice and consultancy on legislation and on the development of financial institutions; and it would consider a financial contribution to the rehabilitation of banks' portfolios where these are weighed down by non-performing loans, although the total sums required for this, with an estimate of over $10 billion for Yugoslavia alone, reach far beyond the Community's PHARE budget.[6]

A third area is the promotion of small and medium enterprises and of the private sector generally. Here the Commission may provide financial assistance for institutions that offer credits to small firms, for arrangements to guarantee such credits, and for organizations that provide services for small and medium enterprises. In Poland there has been a contribution to equity funds for enterprises, to be approved in each case by the European Investment Bank. Another priority is the promotion of inward investment.

A fourth area is 'social', in the sense often used in the Community that relates to questions of employment: labour-market agencies and policies, including particularly training; and social security arrangements.

Beyond these core areas is the establishment of other laws, regulations and services for market economy: laws and regulations for ownership; insurance, accountancy, taxation, competition policy; standards, where harmonization with EC practice is important for both sides; statistics, customs and trade support agencies. There are some forms of assistance intended to strengthen civil society. In Poland these are aimed to improve local government and the participation of associations and interest groups in shaping national and local policies. In Hungary, it is intended that the need to strengthen civil society should be an element across the range of assistance under the PHARE programme, helping to build up the role of local government and of all kinds of non-state bodies, including trade unions, employers' organizations, professional associations, consumer bodies and non-governmental organizations concerned with the environment. Beyond these general requirements for a market economy and pluralist society are a number of sectors in which the Community is ready to offer help, including agriculture, energy, transport and communications, education and health. Should aid for such sectors go beyond technical assistance in seeking to regenerate the physical and social structure, the sums needed could rapidly dwarf the present PHARE budget; and the same is true of aid to improve the environment, which is of major concern to both the Community and the beneficiary countries.

The Community was able to mount this programme expeditiously from the time when the Commission brought together its PHARE Operational Service at the end of 1989, partly because of the experience and knowledge of technical and financial assistance of people coming from the Directorate General VIII, which deals with the Community's development aid. One advantage of Community practice for the beneficiaries is that tenders for goods or services bought with the Community's money are open to offers from any of the twelve member states or the six East European recipients, save only when the sum is being spent on a contract that is too small to justify this procedure. The opening of tenders to such competition has been found to bring substantial saving compared with the tendering under national assistance programmes, which is open only to offers from firms of that nationality.[7] A drawback in providing assistance to the countries of Eastern Europe has, however, been that at present their administrations generally lack the skills to compile a coherent programme, so that when the Commission asks for programmes to assist, it often receives a mere shopping list of projects. Another problem, self-inflicted by the Community, has been that the time-limits imposed by budgetary control have inhibited the support of projects or programmes that may require expenditure beyond a year or two. Thus money approved in the Community's budget for 1990 had to be allocated in that year and spent not later than in 1991 ('non-dissociated expenditure', in the Community jargon). In 1991 this rule was relaxed, so that disbursement could go beyond 1992 (called 'dissociated expenditure'). Efficient aid programmes should be multi-annual. The Community has arranged for this in its European Development Fund for aid to the African, Caribbean and Pacific countries; and financial assistance for the Mediterranean countries is agreed with them in financial protocols to their cooperation agreements, and hence is not subject to the normal time-limits for Community budget spending. If the Community's assistance is really to see the East Europeans through their times of transition, it will have to find a way to commit itself beyond the budgetary allocations so far agreed for 1991 and 1992.

Beyond PHARE

The Commission is seeking to devise a multi-annual 'envelope' for aid to all the PHARE recipient countries which will ensure that there is a global fund to be spent among them over the next four or five years. The allocation for each year would then be divided among them according to the Community's assessment of their absorption capacities and their respective progress with reform. In this way the member states would be committed to a given total effort over the medium term, but the Community would not be tied down to a figure for each recipient, regardless of its circumstances, as would be the case if all the aid were distributed in advance through financial protocols to the agreements with each country. This idea has been adopted in part with respect to the aid to Mediterranean countries for the period 1991–6, with half committed in financial protocols with each country and half in a global commitment.[8] In 1988, the member states as well as the European Parliament accepted for the first time the principle of a 'financial perspective' for expenditure over the next five years, in order to ensure that the agricultural spending would not exceed agreed limits and that the expenditure for 'cohesion', or the contribution to the structural funds in order to help development in the member states with the weaker economies, would not fall below the agreed minimum that is to rise until it reaches ecus 14 billion, or one-third of 1% of Community GDP, in 1993.[9] So a budgetary commitment for five years for aid to the East Europeans would not break new ground; it is anyway proposed that the Community produce a new financial perspective for its budget as a whole for 1993–7.[10] But there remains the question of how big the commitment for East Europeans should be.

The transition from command to market economy is not good news for the balance of payments. There is pressure to import because of the shortfall of resources for consumption and investment, while exports may be limited by time-lags in the supply response to market mechanisms. The collapse of the Comecon trade system has reinforced the pressure to import from the West while at the same time raising costs of exportable goods by increasing the prices of materials, which had been held down far below world levels. In particular, the USSR requires, from the end of 1990, the world price for its oil in hard currency instead of a much lower price in roubles; and on top of that, the Gulf crisis almost doubled the world price for a few critical months. Circumstances have multiplied the size of the problem of financing the balance of payments during the East Europeans' transition.

In 1989, the USSR charged other Comecon countries for its oil at a price equivalent to something between $5 and $10 per barrel in transferable roubles.[11] Now they have to pay in hard currency at a price expected to be at least twice as high. An estimate of the cost in hard currency at world prices, obtained before the Gulf crisis, was $8–10 billion (ecu 6–8 billion) a year.[12]

East European net debt stood at nearly $100 billion at the end of 1990: for Poland $43 billion, Hungary $20 billion, Yugoslavia some $16 billion, Bulgaria $10 billion, Czechoslovakia $7 billion, Romania $1 billion (see Table 4.1). Poland, with a ratio of debt-servicing obligations to convertible currency earnings calculated at 91% in 1989, had suspended the servicing of its debt, so that the interest due was accumulating as new debt. Realizing that this was incompatible with the achievement of a viable economy, the official creditors, who accounted for three-quarters of Poland's total debt, agreed in March 1991 to the writing-off of half or more of the $33 billion owed to them, so that the burden of servicing will be light in the first few years. The ratios between servicing and convertible currency earnings are much lower for Czechoslovakia and Yugoslavia, while Romania has little debt. But the burden for Hungary is still very heavy, with the Hungarians achieving continued servicing in full. While a write-off is inappropriate, the success of Hungary's reforms will be at risk unless something is done to lighten the load. This could take the form of a loan equivalent to, say, half the debt, with interest rates very low or zero for a five-year period, rising after that to market rates. That would enable Hungary to repay half its existing debt, while being exonerated from servicing the new loan during the five years in which, it may be hoped, the transition to a competitive market economy will become assured of success. Something similar will surely have to be done for Bulgaria, the servicing of whose debt, owed, like Hungary's, mainly to the private sector, rose to 80% of convertible currency earnings in 1989, and which on top of that was hard hit by the impact of the Gulf war on its trade with and credits to Iraq.

If such obstacles are surmounted and the reforms begin to succeed, growth should gather pace to a rate of at least 5% a year. The Commission has estimated that, with growth at that rate, the net effect on the balance of payments of Eastern Europe would be negative to the extent of ecu 6.5 billion in 1991, rising to ecu 11 billion in 1995.[13] With the faster growth assumed by the Centre for Economic Policy Research, the gap would be wider.[14] The more dynamic economy should eventually generate exports, and such a deficit would then be reduced or eliminated. But meanwhile, there remains the need to finance the balance of payments during the transition; and until private capital flows in the required quantities, the problem is one for the public authorities.

The Commission estimated the external financing needs of the East European countries at ecu 14 billion for 1991.[15] Provision of ecu 10 billion by the G24 and the international financial institutions was already assured by December 1990, so a further ecu 4 billion would have been required. With the price of oil lower following the Gulf war, the need will be less. But as these economies return to growth they are likely to continue to need such balance-of-payments support until inward private investment really takes off, which may not be until the mid-1990s. Since it is not advisable to add to the burden of servicing debt for most of these countries during that period, the interest on this financing should be subsidized from the budgets of G24 countries, and of the EC in particular.

Unemployment is a nasty part of the medicine that has to be swallowed in the transition to a market economy, and one that the East Europeans, after over four decades without having to take it at all, may be ill-adapted to endure for long. The European market economies all have unemployment assistance and training for new employment in order to deal with the problem in their own countries. In their straitened circumstances, it is hard for East Europeans to finance such programmes adequately. So the Commission had good reason to propose that 'accompanying measures (unemployment insurance, professional retraining and geographical mobility) should be included among the priorities for co-ordinated assistance';[16] and this has particular force in relation to the Central Europeans with their Europe Agreements, because here the Community has a closer interest in the success of the reforms. Without adequate expenditure to mitigate the pain of unemployment and to offer hope for employment in the future, those affected by unemployment could react in ways that would cause the reforms to fail.

Estimates of annual incomes per head in Central Europe vary widely. An average of ecu 1,500 per head may be on the low side.[17] Ecu 1,000 each to finance unemployment assistance and training for the unemployed should not be seen as other than modest. If there are to be two million unemployed Poles by the end of 1991, there may be three million in Central Europe as a whole in the early 1990s. It could go higher. The PHARE programme is providing technical assistance for the necessary agencies and for training those who run them. But it may also be prudent for the donor countries to share the running costs in the early years, to help ensure continued support for the reforms.

There is also the prospect of migrants or refugees. A Polish estimate of the cost of each immigrant from among the million Poles who live in the Soviet Union is equivalent to ecu 1,500 a year until they are absorbed into the Polish economy.[18] Even if the fears that some millions of refugees from the USSR will cross the long frontier with Poland are discounted, the Poles may need help in order to cope; and the same could apply to Hungary, with the two million Hungarians in Romania. The Community, together with some of the Efta countries, could experience a knock-on effect from such migration, intensifying the pressure to move westwards; and high unemployment in Central Europe will certainly cause many Poles and others to wish to seek jobs in the West. Although strict control of immigration may succeed in keeping most of them out, it is not a pleasant process; and it is particularly unpleasant to apply it to countries that are associated with the Community and likely to become candidates for membership. It is in the interest of the Community that life should be made tolerable for their unemployed.

In addition to sustaining the process of reform, the East Europeans face an enormous task of regenerating the physical structure of their economies. One aspect that is crucial for the health of their people is cleaning up the environment. The Community's PHARE programme has begun by assisting them to establish units within their administrations, in order to evaluate the environmental problems and to have the capacity to make and execute policy effectively. At the same time, the PHARE aid is helping them to put an end to some of the worst pollution and to start the process of cleaning up. Ecu 82.5 million of the Community's PHARE aid had been allocated to these purposes up to January 1991.[19] But the capacity for environmental policy that is being created will serve to produce longer-term strategies that will be much more expensive if these countries are to be brought up to Community standards; and it is strongly in the Community's interest that they should be, for existing member states can be severely damaged by cross-frontier pollution. The effect on eastern parts of Germany of the Czech and Polish parts of the 'death triangle' is a case in point; and Chernobyl showed how the damage done by nuclear accidents can carry farther afield. With the Community opening its market to exports from the eastern countries, moreover, free trade can be undermined by competition that is low-cost because of low environmental standards. More immediately, an improvement of some of the appalling pollution and hence of the health of many people in Eastern Europe would vividly demonstrate the benefits of reforms designed to establish pluralist economic and political systems.[20]

The eastern part of Germany indicates the magnitude of the task. The German minister for the environment announced that DM 40 billion (c. ecu 20 billion) would be spent on cleansing the eastern Länder in 1991; and the IFO institute in Munich has estimated that over DM 200 billion will have to be invested before the standards of the Federal Republic are attained.[21] The need for Eastern Europe as a whole must be very much greater.

It has been pointed out that much of the necessary expenditure will consist of the closure of polluting industrial plant that must anyway be replaced because it has depended on unrealistically low energy prices and is technologically obsolescent.[22] This does not diminish the urgency of the environmental task, while it does augment its economic desirability. It means that a large part of the spending to improve the environment can be subsumed within the process of regenerating the physical structure as a whole. This brings us back to the question of the total investment outlays for that broad purpose, which were put by the Centre for Economic Policy Research at $103–226 billion (ecu 85–190 billion) a year for Central and Eastern Europe, excluding Yugoslavia.[23] Although the wide spread from top to bottom of that estimate reflects the authors' wise abstention from any pretension to accuracy, the World Bank's figure for the cost of investment required for the same countries in telecommunications alone, at $60 billion (ecu 50 billion) over a ten- to twelve-year period, indicates that the order of magnitude is not wide of the mark.[24] Most of the investment should be undertaken by private capital. But some, such as roads and part of the environmental clean-up, consists of public goods for which private capital will not be forthcoming. In view of the strain on the budgets of reforming countries during the first few years of their reforms, there is a strong case for western assistance for such expenditure beyond the amounts allocated so far for the first three years of the PHARE programme, which suffice for technical assistance but not much more. To this should be added the case made earlier for help with unemployment pay and for relieving the burden of servicing debt and finance for balance-of-payments support over the next few years. The main purpose of aid must, however, be to get the reforming countries onto the path of self-sustaining growth to the point at which their need for inward investment will be entirely looked after by private capital; so the amount of aid should be enough not only to sustain the reforms but also to create the momentum that will draw the necessary private capital along with it. There is no precise way to estimate this amount. But it may be surmised that it is closer to the ecu 14 billion mentioned by President Delors than to the sums that the Community, as the principal G24 donor, is at present providing.[25]

Completing Marshall Aid?

The analogy with Marshall Aid has been much discussed.[26] It has indeed been heavily criticized; and there are substantial differences. One is that six years of war for market economies are not the same as four decades in which the market system has been thoroughly destroyed. Thus the West Europeans who received the Marshall Aid could be expected to recover in four years, whereas East Europeans will need more time. But they are nevertheless expected to recover. That is the aim of the aid and the association agreements. The difference is that the process will take longer; and in the first years their capacity to absorb aid productively is likely to be less. There are sharp variations among them in their absorption capacities: the Central Europeans can absorb more help sooner.[27] But the prospect that they too will take longer than West Europeans did to recover does not seem to tell against the Marshall Plan as a useful metaphor.

A second difference is that Marshall Aid came from only two donors, the US and Canada, and went to a group of the West European states acting for some purposes collectively, whereas in the present case it is the donors that are acting collectively, and there are strong arguments against requiring East Europeans to form a common organization to receive the aid. In the short term, the administrations in some of the countries are still too weak to cope with the extra complication of such an organization, particularly since there is so much diversity among them; and it is doubtful whether a sub-regional group is a serious long-term aim for any of them, whereas it was the long-term prospect of unification among West European countries that gave much of the merit to the common organization for the Marshall Plan. East Europeans have made it clear that their long-term aim is membership of the Community, which, it was suggested earlier, will be the Community's interest too.

A sub-regional group would therefore have to be justified for its usefulness in the shorter term. Because the level of development of the Central Europeans is more advanced, the most feasible such group would be confined to them; and the leaders of Czechoslovakia, Hungary and Poland did indeed discuss the possibility of an 'open free-trade zone' when they met in February 1991.[28] But they may not pursue this idea very zealously. Their main concern is to align their economies on world-market prices. Free trade among them could, instead, require adjustments based on the competition from one or other of their own pricing systems, each with its different irrational starting-point. The pain and cost of mutual adjustment would be worth while only if their prices were well on the way to being based on the rationale of the market economy, by which time they will be near to opening their markets to Community exporters under the Europe Agreements.

The idea of a sub-regional payments union for the Central Europeans has, as we have seen, likewise been overtaken by their desire, shared by the other East European countries, to achieve international convertibility. The value of cooperation among East European countries is political rather than economic: that it should help to overcome the animosities that have plagued relations between these nations in the past. Cooperation on specific matters should help to serve this purpose, and the Community's PHARE programme seeks to promote it through what has been termed its 'regional window': assistance provided on a regional basis where there is a scale economy, as for example with training facilities for the development of standards and of statistics, and with policies for energy-saving and nuclear safety; or programmes that involve joint planning such as the TEMPUS (Transeuropean Mobility Programme for University Studies) programme for exchanges in higher education. In general, however, the aid for Eastern Europe does not require a collective response that would lead towards unification of the group.

More to the point is the original aim of the Marshall Plan, to promote the unification of the European countries as a whole. The East Europeans were left out of the process through Stalin's fiat. It has been suggested that their omission leaves unfinished business in the form of a 'completion' of the Marshall Plan which would lead to their integration in the European Community;[29] and that, like the original Marshall Plan, this would respond to the connection between economic need and political danger.[30] Similarly, again, the commitment of donors to a multi-annual programme would reflect the need for some consistency in seeing through the process of recovery, as had been recognized in the Commission's preference for a 'multi-annual envelope': the need, indeed, for a certain constancy and generosity of approach if the challenge of the transformation of Eastern Europe is to be properly met. It is hard to avoid the suspicion that much of the criticism of the Marshall Aid metaphor amounted to rejection of the idea of doing something generous, whether in its total scale or in the proportion of grants to loans – with grants accounting for four-fifths of Marshall Aid, compared with one-quarter to the PHARE programme so far, if the contributions to the BERD are included.

Marshall Aid was, as a *Financial Times* leader expressed it, 'a benchmark for what generous assistance could amount to'.[31] The 1.3% of US gross national product authorized in a period of less than four years between 1948 and 1952 would comprise, for the Community today, an annual rate of over ecu 50 billion. The one-third of 1% of GDP indicated by President Delors (ecu 14 billion) or the one-quarter of 1% suggested by the French Foreign Minister De Michelis (ecu 10 billion) are far from extravagant in comparison;[32] and they are modest compared with the extra public-sector deficit equivalent to 3% of GDP that the Federal Republic is incurring on behalf of the eastern Länder in 1991. Of course it does not follow that, because the US gave a certain percentage of its GDP in 1948–52, the EC should give the same proportion now. But its political leaders would show a shameful lack, not just of generosity but of ability to grasp the essentials of enlightened self-interest, if they were unable to see that the needs of Eastern Europe may call, over the next five years, for a substantially larger aid programme than the present one. The Community should at least consider how much aid the eastern countries could usefully absorb, not just this year and next, when their absorption capacity is still likely to be limited, but over a longer period when their regeneration is really under way. If inward private investment takes off faster than expected, the aid requirement will be reduced. It is more likely that political leaders, confronted by estimates of the aid that would be enough to ensure the success of the reforms in the absence of such a response from the private sector, will feel that they are not up to the job of delivering it. But the matter is important enough to justify the effort to secure an adequate commitment from the Community, not just in 1991 and 1992, but through at least the first years of a financial perspective for the Community budget from 1993 to 1997.

The earlier discussion of the various elements of aid indicated that the total size of an adequate programme is more likely to be in double than in single figures of billions of ecus. How much is required from the Community budget depends on the division between the EC and the other G24 countries; but the Community will have to bear the brunt. It also depends on the proportions of grants and of loans in the aid programme. Loans in the first years must in any case be on terms that require budgetary subvention, because additions to the burden of servicing debt would be self-defeating. But it would be feasible to offer much of the aid in the form of loans that are interest-free for a grace period of, say, five years or more, thus reducing the call on the public purse to the amount of the interest-rate subsidies. Such loans on a large scale would, however, leave the recipients at the end of that period weighed down by debt, from which Marshall Aid, with its high proportion of grants, exonerated the West Europeans. The Central Europeans are likely by then to be entering the second phase of their Europe Agreements, hence beginning to open their markets in earnest to the Community. It is greatly preferable that they should not then have their economies burdened by debt. The case for a high proportion of grants is strong; and such a case has already prevailed for the beneficiaries from the European Development Fund under the Lomé Convention, who are receiving over 90% of their aid during the current five-year period in the form of grants. In so far as the grants can be used by the recipients to pay the cost of local goods and services, moreover, it will be possible for East European countries to apply the aid ecus towards debt reduction.

Germany gave a strong impulse to the launching of the Community's policy towards the reforming countries of Eastern Europe, and to the aid programme in particular. Not only has Germany the keenest interest in its neighbours to the East, but, when German unification became possible, the government of the Federal Republic deemed it of the utmost importance to foster good relations with all concerned, including the Soviet Union and Central Europeans. But Germany is now preoccupied with the enormous task of raising the eastern Länder to the level of the western ones. If a new wave of Community eastern policy is needed in order to ensure an adequate aid programme over the medium term as well as to open the Community market where it will benefit the eastern partners most, the responsibility for initiating it will lie elsewhere. The result, in terms of stable and prosperous eastern partners, is in the general interest of Community countries. Securing German participation in a Community policy, rather than a Germany that acts on its own, is also in the interest of Germany's partners, Britain included. It is to be hoped that Britain's influence in launching a new phase of Community policy will be at least as positive as it was in promoting the idea of association.

Assisting the Soviet Union

The European Council decided in December 1991 that the Community should extend its aid to the East with a substantial programme for the Soviet Union. This aid got off to a bad start, not only because of the Community's reaction against repression in the Baltic republics, but also because the Soviet authorities, having initially accepted that the food aid could be conveyed direct to the bodies that would distribute it locally, insisted in January 1991 that it should go only to central stores, which, given the state of the Soviet distribution system, was not acceptable to the Community. Ways can be found through such bureaucratic problems, which do not in any case arise in connection with the ecu 500 million of guaranteed credits for food exports from the Community to the Soviet

Union, for which more commercial criteria apply and with which the Soviet authorities buy and dispose of the food under their own responsibility. It is up to the Community, however, to determine where they may buy it from. It was proposed, following the Community's practice in the PHARE programme, that purchases could be made not only in the Community but also in the East European countries; and the Community could make its East European policy as well as its aid to the Soviet Union more effective by extending the PHARE practice in this way.

For the technical assistance programme of ecu 400 million, likewise suspended following the Baltic repressions, the Community defined five priorities reflecting Soviet needs: management training, financial institutions, transport, energy, and distribution of food products.[33] As with the British Know-How Fund of £20 million for the Soviet Union for 1991 and 1992, most of the money was to be spent on training, with some allowance for equipment such as computers. A valuable by-product of training programmes, particularly those that bring Soviet people to Community countries, will be the personal contacts of which so many Soviet people have been deprived for so long; and extension of the TEMPUS programme for higher education exchanges would serve this purpose too. Indeed, if friendly relations continue between the Community and the Soviet Union, it might be worth while to consider, as a separate project, a programme of youth exchanges such as did so much to cement Franco-German relations in the postwar period.

Since technical assistance lacks the humanitarian dimension of food aid, it is more sensitive to political conditions. But, provided that there is neither a crisis in political relations nor flagrant violation of human rights, the main condition for the provision of technical assistance is that of effectiveness: the aid should be usefully applied. It need not be conditional on prior achievement of progress towards economic reform. Its purpose is, rather, to facilitate reform; and if the Soviet regime does not prevent the aid from acting as a facilitator, the aid should be provided – although the case for a larger programme becomes stronger as reform proceeds. The Community's offer of ecu 400 million has been criticized on the grounds that the Soviet Union could not usefully absorb so much at present. But a start can be made with the sum that can be absorbed, with the flow increasing as the absorption capacity rises. The question of absorption capacity becomes more acute if the larger sums involved in financial assistance are contemplated.

A credible programme of economic reform would be another condition for providing larger sums of financial assistance. The Soviet Union is likely to need balance-of-payments support in 1991; and proposals for convertibility may remain on the agenda. The IMF, well informed about the Soviet economy since completing, together with other international institutions, the report on the Soviet economy late in 1990, would pose macroeconomic policy conditions for according its support.[34] In mid-1990, when hopes for radical reform in the Soviet Union were high, the West was considering the question of aid to encourage the reform effort more generally. Subsequent events induced a more pessimistic reappraisal. The Community should certainly be prepared for the worst. But it should also be ready to seize the opportunity if a convincing reform programme is launched to develop a market system including the appropriate monetary, financial and fiscal institutions, private and independent enterprises, and price determination. In July 1990, *The Financial Times* suggested that $50 billion or more would have to be provided by the West in order to give such a reform an adequate chance to succeed; by May 1991, with comprehensive reform again on the agenda, estimates of an appropriate sum, based in part on the report of the IMF and others, ranged from $10 billion a year upwards.[35] As with East Europeans, a major purpose of such official aid would be to draw along behind it a healthy flow of private capital. The scope for investment in the energy sector was indicated in Chapter 6; and such private investment, which may need public support for a part of the risk, would do much to stimulate the domestic economy and to link it with the international economy. Given a fair prospect for reforms, the Community should consider providing substantial further aid to consolidate the process. One field for it could be the environment. While estimates of the cost of cleaning it are still rudimentary, the suggestion that well over roubles 200 billion would be needed is not excessive in comparison with the estimated costs of cleaning the environment in the eastern German Länder.[36] If the Community is to be able to fulfil its political and economic objectives with respect to the Soviet Union, it needs the capacity to make a major contribution to such programmes.

Conditions for aid

If people are starving, the only condition for food aid is that it should reach them. If there is a shortage of food but not starvation, there can be added the condition that such aid should not be used to bolster a repressive regime which is in flagrant contravention of human rights. A further condition may be added that concerns the Community, not its eastern neighbours. The food aid should not be given at the expense of starving people in the world's South. Representatives of southern countries have expressed concern about such diversion; and they should be reassured that it will not occur. It is also desirable that southern countries should not lose aid in general because of the programmes for the East. The regeneration of the reforming countries in Europe is an investment that will benefit Europe as a whole, and does not detract from the case for aid to the South.

The principal condition for assistance at present levels is effectiveness. The money must not be thrown into black holes where it is wasted. Nor, since it is intended to assist the creation of market economies and eventually pluralist democracies, should substantial sums be spent on countries whose regimes are bent on blocking the transition to market economy or suppressing any manifestations of civil society. Nor should aid bolster regimes that are hostile to the Community and the West. But, given those conditions, assistance can be provided where there is a good chance that it will facilitate the process of economic reform. Financial assistance on a larger scale should depend, like the negotiation of the Europe Agreements, on hard evidence of serious efforts to carry through a programme of reform to achieve market economy and pluralist democracy.

This underlines the importance of the Community's capacity to judge such evidence. Not only will the success of the Europe Agreements or of a *grand accord* with the Soviet Union depend on it, but so also would decisions to allocate larger sums for aid. The assessment of progress with, and prospects for, reforms should enable the Community to distribute its aid to the best effect among the recipient countries and, in agreement with their governments, within them. This may lead to some differentiation among the countries that are still at the stage of trade and cooperation agreements. But the principal effect could be to increase considerably the aid for those countries with a convincing prospect of completing the transition to competitive market economy and solid pluralist democracy: that is, in the first instance, Czechoslovakia, Hungary and Poland. The Community should at the same time be prepared to extend the list to include others that may follow them, and in particular to respond positively to favourable developments in the Soviet Union.

8

AN EASTERN POLICY
FOR THE COMMUNITY

The preceding chapters have considered what policies the Community might pursue to further its interests in the establishment of competitive market economies and stable pluralist democracies among its neighbours to the East, and in constructive relations with them.

Europe Agreements are the focus for the countries of Central Europe: Hungary, Poland, and Czechoslovakia. In moving towards a free trade relationship with them, the Community has some hard decisions to take to liberalize its imports of agricultural products, coal, steel and textiles, and to increase the employment opportunities it offers to their people. The Community has shown itself ready to support their efforts to sustain convertibility and can encourage them to peg their currencies to the ecu, moving eventually to their participation in an exchange-rate mechanism. A big flow of private investment into their economies is an essential objective; and before that takes hold, substantial aid is required, probably much more than hitherto. In order to apply such aid to the best effect – to be sure that the association continues to be justified by their progress towards completing their pluralist democracy and market economy and, when the time comes that they apply to join the Community, that completion has been solidly achieved – the Community will need a strong capacity to assess the Associates' political and economic situations. It must be open to any European country that wants to join and has a solid pluralist democracy and working market economy. But it would be dangerous to accept members that have not fulfilled these conditions. It seems likely that the Central Europeans will do so in the 1990s. So also may Yugoslavia, or at least its northwestern republics if they become independent. For other East Europeans, the following decade is a more likely time. Meanwhile, the Community will have to develop its relation-ships with them, starting with the trade and cooperation agreements and the PHARE aid and liberalization, but upgrading those to Europe Agree-ments when they have embarked on convincing programmes of reform.

The Community has a powerful interest in Soviet reforms, the more so because of the implications for security. But the process of reform is more problematic than in the Central European countries, and less open to influence by the Community. The Community should be able to apply the whole range of its external economic policy instruments in relation to the Soviet Union, with the possibility some time in the coming years of aid on a large scale, and with Community involvement in the framework for major agreements in the energy sector. In the wider field of foreign policy, the Community needs to be ready to cooperate closely with a Soviet Union that is moving towards democracy, but also to respond to the dangers that could stem from disintegration of the Soviet Union or from an authoritarian regime. In order to cope with these challenges, the Com-munity should adopt more effective ways of forming common foreign policies, and member states need to construct a European pillar within Nato as the American contribution to European security diminishes.

Implications for the Community
The Community's instruments of trade policy are on the whole adequate for what it has to do in relation to the East. It has to revise its anti-dumping regulation so that the normal procedure for market econo-mies replaces the more arbitrary one for state-trading countries as the reforming countries move towards market systems. There is a good case for strengthening Community control of the terms of export credits, in order to prevent uneconomic and unfair competition among the member states in their use of this powerful tool of export promotion, as well as for Community involvement in application of the CoCom controls, as a logical consequence of the single-market programme. The Community may also need some new instruments to implement the energy charter.

To place its aid to the eastern countries on a stable footing, the Community should allocate in a 'financial perspective' for its budget 1993–7 an adequate sum, which may have to be considerably larger than the PHARE programme at present. Flexibility is desirable, both for allocation of expenditure between different years and for the division of the aid among countries. The ecu, which is likely to become the Com-munity's currency under the treaty resulting from the Intergovernmental

Conference on economic and monetary union, will have an important role in relation to the eastern countries. It is also relevant that a major reason for French insistence on the single currency is the expectation that this would anchor Germany more firmly in the Community and thus help to ensure that Germany does not play an increasingly independent role in the East. This is also a motive behind the French support for more majority voting in the making of a common foreign policy, which is backed by Germany, too, with its desire for a strong Community political framework. Nor will the Community's explicit aim of a 'European foreign policy' (art. 30 SEA), which is particularly important in relation to the Soviet Union and Eastern Europe, be adequately realized unless its institutions are strengthened.

In order to have an effective eastern policy, the Community may need to act quickly, decisively and coherently, which it has often failed to do in the past. It needs to provide the strong framework for Germany that the Germans themselves want, conscious of their exposed position in the centre of Europe. It also needs institutions strong enough to contain the Central and eventually other East European countries when they are ready to join, as well as those Efta members that wish to apply for membership, without undermining its capacity for action.

Majority voting in the Council is appropriate for much of the Community's eastern policy. For the Germans, it can bring the whole weight of the Community more efficiently behind the policy, thus ensuring that they do not have to bear the brunt of the responsibility and of the provision of funds; for Germany's Community partners, it should diminish fears that the Germans would be tempted to pursue the policy of 'strongest alone'.[1] As the Community becomes enlarged, moreover, to include first the Eftans, then Central Europeans, then other East Europeans, and the number of member states thus grows from twelve to fifteen, then to twenty and perhaps eventually twenty-five, the procedure of unanimity will become less and less practicable. Majority voting will have to become the general rule at an early stage in that process.

The European Parliament already has the power of co-legislation with the Council for the Community's most important decisions about its relations with the East Europeans: for the enactment of treaties of association and of accession, and for the approval of budgetary provision for aid. If difficulty over these key decisions is to be avoided, the Parliament will have to be satisfied with the conduct of the relationship with the eastern countries by the Council and the Commission. *De facto*, this will not work smoothly without co-decision with respect to the relationship as

a whole. *De jure*, the Federal Republic has proposed to the Intergovernmental Conference on political union that co-legislation be the general
procedure where the Council will vote by majority for the enactment of
Community law. Chancellor Kohl has made it clear that the German
government regards such steps towards political union as a necessary
part of the package that includes economic and monetary union.[2] Attempts to untie that package carry the risk that Germany will not feel
bound to set the development of its future policy towards the East within
a Community framework.

With growth in the scope of the PHARE programme and technical
assistance for the Soviet Union, the Commission's capacity to assess the
aid needs of the eastern neighbours, and to disburse that aid effectively,
calls for urgent strengthening; and this goes along with its need to build
up the capacity to judge economic and political developments in those
countries as a basis for major decisions of Community policy. This in
turn is a particular instance of the general case for the Commission to
have adequate staff to make proper use of the right of initiative in matters
of Community foreign policy that is likely to emerge from the Intergovernmental Conference on political union, in order to link the Community's powers in external economic policy more effectively with other
aspects of foreign policy.[3]

There is wide agreement that a European defence pillar within Nato
should be built around the WEU. But there are differences among the
member governments about its relationship with the Community. While
care has to be taken not to undermine the transatlantic relationship, it
must also be recognized that if Community policy towards the East is to
be fully effective, it will be necessary to link its economic and security
aspects more closely together.

There are grounds, then, for strengthening the Community's powers
and institutions in order to conduct a more effective eastern policy. That
might not be sufficient to make the case for 'deepening' the Community
if arguments relating to other fields of Community activity pointed in the
opposite direction. This is not the place to consider the general case for
strengthening the Community. The present writer's view that policy
towards the East is but one example of this general case is explained
elsewhere.[4] The conclusion, with respect both to the general case and to
the particular example considered in this paper, is that the IGCs in 1991
should strengthen the Community's powers in relation to foreign and
security policy as well as economic and monetary union, and should
reform the institutions in favour of more majority voting in the Council,

a stronger role for the European Parliament and a reinforcement of the Commission.

These reforms would enable the Community to conduct a more powerful eastern policy and provide a stronger framework for the united Germany. But such deepening should not be seen as a means of excluding East Europeans. It should, on the contrary, be part of a two-pronged strategy, whose other half is the widening of the Community until it includes all democratic European states that wish to join, as most of them almost certainly will during the course of the next two decades. In order to ensure that such a Community is workable as well as democratic, the political union should be completed during the 1990s, in particular by making majority voting the general rule in the Council and co-legislation the general procedure for enactment of laws. Meanwhile, the Community should use all the instruments of its eastern policy to support democracy and the market economy among the eastern countries and to establish a stable and balanced relationship with the Soviet Union. It is strongly against the Community's interest to allow protectionist pressures to undermine the success of this policy. It is likewise important that preoccupation with Europe should not be to the detriment of the Community's wider interests, including its policies of trade and aid with respect to the less-developed countries of the South.

For most of the past four decades, British policy has run counter, first to the creation, then to the deepening of the Community. This policy has been carried through to the IGCs, with British opposition to the single currency, to more majority voting in the Council, to a stronger legislative role for the European Parliament, and to institutional links between the WEU and the Community. This study of the Community's relations with Eastern Europe and the Soviet Union suggests that such reluctance to strengthen the Community can only weaken the development of the Community's eastern policy as well as the prospects for a successful enlargement to the East, and hence defeat the purposes of the British government's own positive eastern policy. In so far as Britain does manage to prevent the deepening of the Community, moreover, the result is likely to be increasingly independent action on the part of Germany in relations with the East. In none of this would British interests be served. The British government would do well, instead, to promote a strategy of deepening as well as widening, with the Community using its growing strength to consolidate pluralist democracy and the market economy in Central Europe, to encourage their development in the rest of Eastern Europe and the Soviet Union, and to put its considerable weight behind the establishment of a secure and peaceful Europe and wider world.

NOTES

Chapter 1

1 Centre for Economic Policy Research, *Monitoring European Integration: The Impact of Eastern Europe*, London, CEPR, 1990.

2 Paolo Cecchini with Michel Catinat and Alexis Jacquemin, *The European Challenge 1992: The Benefits of a Single Market*, Aldershot, Wildwood House, 1988.

3 *Resolutions of the Congress of Europe, The Hague 1948*, Brussels, European Movement, reprinted 1988.

4 Dr Otto Storf, *Business Risks and Opportunities in Eastern Europe and the Soviet Union*, paper for Seventh Annual Conference of the Centre for European Policy Studies, 14–16 November 1990, Brussels, CEPS, 1990.

5 Bundeskanzler Dr Helmut Kohl, 'Die Rolle Deutschlands in Europa', speech in Berlin, 13 March 1991.

6 See for example Hanns W. Maull and Achim von Heynitz, 'Osteuropa: Durchbruch in die Postmoderne?: Umrisse einer Strategie des Westens', *Europa-Archiv*, 15/1990.

7 Berndt von Staden, 'Das vereinigte Deutschland in Europa', *Europa-Archiv*, 23/1990, p. 688.

8 Françoise de La Serre, 'La Politique de la Communauté Européenne vis à vis de l'Est: vers une approche globale?', paper for colloquium organized at Bordeaux, 4–6 October 1990, by the Commission pour l'Etude des Communautés Européennes (CEDECE), p. 16. The paper is to be published in *Les relations Communauté Européenne – Europe de l'Est*, Jean-Claude Gautron (ed.), Paris, Economica, forthcoming 1991.

9 Von Staden, 'Das vereinigte Deutschland in Europa' (n. 7, above), pp. 686, 690.

10 *The Financial Times*, 20 March 1990.

11 'Nota over de europese politieke unie', *Tweede Kamer 1990–1991*, 20596, no. 32, 26 October 1991, p. 24.

12 Rt Hon. Margaret Thatcher MP, 'Shaping a New Global Community', speech to the Aspen Institute, Aspen, Colorado, August 1990; and speech to the Federal Assembly, Prague, 18 September 1990.

Chapter 2

1 See text of '17 theses' by the Institute of World Economy and International Relations (IMEMO), Moscow, in *Mirovaya ekonomika i mezhdunarodnye otnosheniye*, (hereafter *MEMO*), 1/1957, and *Kommunist*, 9/1957.

2 '32 theses' by IMEMO, in *MEMO*, 9/1962, and *Pravda*, 26 August 1962.

3 See Alastair Forsyth, *Steel Pricing Policies*, London, Political and Economic Planning (PEP), 1964, pp. 350–2; John and Pauline Pinder, *The European Community's Policy towards Eastern Europe*, European Series no. 25, London, PEP and the Royal Institute of International Affairs (RIIA), 1975, p. 18.

4 *Agence Europe*, 28/29 October 1974. For this and the subsequent period of Community policy, see John Maslen, 'The European Community's Relations with the State–Trading Countries 1981–83', *Yearbook of European Law*, 1983, pp. 323–46, and John Pinder, 'European Integration and East–West Trade: Conflict of Interests or Comedy of Errors?', *Journal of Common Market Studies*, September 1977.

5 See Michael Kaser, *Comecon: Integration Problems of the Planned Economies*, London, Oxford University Press for RIIA, 1967 (1st edn 1965).

6 *Comprehensive Programme for the Further Extension and Improvement of Cooperation and the Development of Socialist Economic Integration by the CMEA Member-Countries*, Moscow, CMEA Secretariat, 1971.

7 See M. M. Maximova, *Osnovnye Problemy Imperialisticheskoy Integratsii*, Moscow, Mysl, 1971; Y. V. Shishkov, *Obschiy Rynok: Nadezhdy i Deistvitelnost*, Moscow, Mysl, 1972; John Pinder, 'Soviet Views of Western Economic Integration', in Avi Shlaim and G. N. Yannopoulos (eds.), *The EEC and Eastern Europe*, Cambridge, Cambridge University Press, 1978.

8 Leonid Brezhnev, speech to 15th Soviet Trade Union Congress, March 1972.

9 John Maslen, 'The European Community's Relations with the State–Trading Countries of Europe 1984–86', *Yearbook of European Law*, 1986, p. 337.

10 For Community agreements with Yugoslavia, see Patrick F. R. Artisien and Stephen Holt, 'Yugoslavia and the EEC in the 1970s', *Journal of Common Market Studies*, June 1980; Will Bartlett and Milica Uvalic, *Yugoslavia and*

EEC Trade Relations: Problems and Prospects, EUI Colloquium Papers, Florence, European University Institute, 1985; Eberhard Rhein, 'Die Europäische Gemeinschaft und das Mittelmeer', *Europa-Archiv*, 22/1986; Oskar Kovac, 'Les relations entre la Yugoslavie et la CEE', *Cadmos*, Geneva, spring 1988.

11 Kovac, 'Les relations entre la Yugoslavie' (n. 10, above), p. 83.

12 *The Financial Times*, 24 February 1982.

13 For EC–Comecon relations in this period, see Maslen, 'The European Community's Relations' (n. 9, above).

14 *Official Journal of the European Community* (hereafter *OJ*) 1984 L/201, cit. in Maslen, ibid., p. 345.

Chapter 3

1 *Pravda*, 16 June 1984, cit. in Maslen, 'The European Community's Relations' (ch. 2, n. 9), p. 336. This source gives a full account of Community policy towards Eastern Europe in the mid-1980s. For the remainder of the decade, see Bernhard May, 'Normalisierung der Beziehungen zwischen der EG und dem RGW', in *Aus Politik und Zeitgeschichte*, supplement to *Der Parlament*, 13 January 1989; Georg Link, *Ungleiche Partner im europäischen Haus: Europäische Gemeinschaft und Rat für Gegenseitige Wirtschaftshilfe*, Bonn, Europa Union Verlag, 1990, pp. 33–7; Christian Lequesne, 'Les accords de commerce et de coopération Communauté européenne – Pays d'Europe de l'Est', paper for CEDECE to be published in Gautron (ed.), *Les relations Communauté Européenne* (ch. 1, n. 8).

2 See Hans-Joachim Seeler, 'Die Beziehungen zwischen der Europäischen Gemeinschaft und dem Rat für Gegenseitige Wirtschaftshilfe', *Europa-Archiv*, 7/1987, p. 190.

3 Speech on receiving Prime Minister Craxi, 29 May 1985.

4 May, 'Normalisierung der Beziehungen' (n. 1, above), p. 46.

5 Statement by Willy De Clercq to the European Parliament, 23 October 1985, *OJ*, Annex no. 2–331, pp. 123–5.

6 For a review of the agreements, see Lequesne, 'Les accords de commerce' (n. 1, above).

7 See Christian Lequesne, 'La RDA et la Communauté Européenne', in Henri Ménudier (ed.), *La RDA 1949–1990: du Stalinisme à la liberté*, Paris, Publications de l'Institut d'Allemand, Université de la Sorbonne Nouvelle–Paris III, 1990.

8 Lequesne, 'Les accords de commerce' (n. 1, above), p. 13.

9 Ibid., p. 9.

10 Commission of the EC, *Action Plan: Coordinated assistance from the Group of 24 to Bulgaria, Czechoslovakia, the German Democratic Republic, Romania and Yugoslavia*, SEC(90)843 final, Brussels, 2 May 1990.

11 G24 Coordination Unit, Directorate General for External Affairs, Brussels, *PHARE Scoreboard*, Commission of the EC, 30 January 1991.
12 Exchange of letters between Poland and the Community, *OJ*, L69/1990, 16 March 1990.
13 Commission of the EC, *XXIIIrd General Report on the Activities of the European Communities 1989*, Brussels, 1990, p. 367.
14 See Lequesne, 'Les accords de commerce' (n. 1, above), pp. 6–8, and de La Serre, 'La Politique de la Communauté Européenne' (ch. 1, n. 8), p. 6.
15 *The Financial Times*, 22 December 1989.
16 Commission of the EC, *Association agreements with the countries of central and eastern Europe: a general outline*, Communication from the Commission to the Council and Parliament, COM(90)398 final, Brussels, 27 August 1990.
17 de La Serre, 'La Politique de la Communauté Européenne' (ch. 1, n. 8), p. 4.
18 Ibid., pp. 3ff.
19 See Link, *Ungleiche Partner im europäischen Haus* (n. 1, above), pp. 34–5.
20 EP 425/74 (Klepsch report on EC relations with East European countries and CMEA), 1–424/81 (De Clercq, East European countries and CMEA), 1–531/82 (Irmer, East European countries and CMEA), A2–111/85 (Bettiza, Central and Eastern Europe), A2–187/86 (Seeler, CMEA and East European countries), A2–155/88 (Hänsch, Soviet Union), A3–22/90 (Walter, Poland), A3–172/90 (Penders, Central–Eastern Europe and Soviet Union), A3–183/90 (Donnelly, German unification), A3–193/90 (Habsburg, Hungary), A3–4/91 (Langer, Albania), A3–55/91 (Randzio–Plath, association agreements).
21 See John Pinder, *European Community: The Building of a Union*, Oxford and New York, Oxford University Press, 1991.
22 See *Agence Europe*, Europe Documents, 29 June 1990, cit. in de La Serre, 'La Politique de la Communauté Européenne' (ch. 1, n. 8), p. 14.

Chapter 4

1 *Association agreements* (ch. 3, n. 165), and *Action Plan* (ch. 3, n. 10).
2 For fuller treatment of East European political reforms, see Garton Ash, *We the People: The Revolution of '89*, Cambridge, Granta Books, 1990; Judy Batt, *East Central Europe from Reform to Transformation*, Chatham House Paper, London, RIIA/Pinter, 1991; Ralf Dahrendorf, *Reflections on the Revolution in Europe*, London, Chatto & Windus, 1990; Mark Frankland, *The Patriots' Revolution: How East Europe won its Freedom*, London, Sinclair-Stevens, 1990; Misha Glenny, *The Rebirth of History: Eastern Europe in the Age of Democracy*, London, Penguin, 1990. For studies on the Soviet Union in the late 1980s, see Archie Brown (ed.), *Political Leadership in the Soviet Union*, London, Macmillan, 1989; Geoffrey

Hosking, *The Awakening of the Soviet Union*, London, Heinemann, 1990; Neil Malcolm, *Soviet Policy Perspectives on Western Europe*, Chatham House Paper, London, RIIA/Pinter, 1989; Stephen White, *Gorbachev in Power*, Cambridge, Cambridge University Press, 1990. For economic reforms, see n. 14 below.

3 *Association agreements* (ch. 3, n. 16).

4 Edward Shils, 'The Virtue of Civil Society', *Government and Opposition*, winter 1991, p. 93. See also Hosking, *The Awakening of the Soviet Union* (n. 2, above), particularly Chapter 4, 'A civil society in embryo'.

5 See Judy Batt, 'Political Reform in Hungary', *Parliamentary Affairs*, October 1990, p. 475.

6 See Dahrendorf, *Reflections on the Revolution in Europe* (n. 2, above), pp. 104–8.

7 See Glenny, *The Rebirth of History* (n. 2, above), p. 234.

8 *The Independent*, 29 January 1991.

9 *The Economist*, 12 January 1991; *The Financial Times*, 9 and 18 January 1991.

10 *Association agreements* (ch. 3, n. 16).

11 Hosking, *The Awakening of the Soviet Union* (n. 2, above), p. 75.

12 'The Soviet Union', Survey, *The Economist*, 20 October 1990, p. 19.

13 Shils, 'The Virtue of Civil Society' (n. 4, above), pp. 5–8.

14 For example, Commission of the EC, 'Economic Transformation in Hungary and Poland', *European Economy no. 43*, March 1990, and 'Stabilization, Liberalization and Devaluation: Assessment of the Economic Situation and Reform Process in the Soviet Union', *European Economy no. 45*, December 1990; Jean-Paul Fitoussi (ed.), *A l'Est, en Europe: Des économies en transition*, Paris, Presses de la Fondation Nationale des Sciences Politiques, 1990; International Monetary Fund, World Bank, OECD, European Bank for Reconstruction and Development, *The Economy of the USSR: Summary and Recommendations*, Washington, World Bank, 1990; J. M. C. Rollo with Judy Batt, Brigitte Granville and Neil Malcolm, *The New Eastern Europe: Western Responses*, Chatham House Paper, RIIA/Pinter, 1990; Jeffrey Sachs, 'Eastern Europe's Economies: What is to be done?', *The Economist*, 13 January 1990; Julian Schweitzer, 'Transition in Eastern Europe – The Social Dimension', and Willi Wapenhaus, 'The Challenge of Economic Reforms in Eastern Europe', *Finance and Development*, December 1990; UN Economic Commission for Europe (UNECE), *Economic Survey of Europe in 1990–1991*, New York, United Nations, 1991, pp. 122–34.

15 See Lawrence J. Brainard, *Reform in Eastern Europe: Creating a Capital Market*, AMEX Bank Review Special Paper no. 18, London, American Express Bank Ltd, November 1990.

16 See Richard Portes, *The Transition to Convertibility for Eastern Europe*

and the USSR, Discussion Paper no. 500, London, CEPR, January 1991.

17 CEPR, *Monitoring European Integration* (ch. 1, n. 1), pp. 38–9.

18 For example, David Gros and Alfred Steinherr, 'Problems, Differences and Similarities in Central Europe and the Soviet Union', paper for CEPS conference, Brussels, Centre for European Policy Studies, 14–16 November 1990; Richard Portes, 'Introduction', *European Economy no. 43*, March 1990; Sachs, 'Eastern Europe's Economies' (n. 14, above).

19 UNECE, *Economic Survey of Europe* (n. 14, above). Unless otherwise stated, the statistics in the following text are derived from this source.

20 Ibid., Tables 2.2.6, 2.2.14.

21 *The Financial Times*, 16 January 1991; 'Eastern Europe in Transition', Survey, *The Financial Times*, 4 February 1991, p. 15.

22 CEPR, *Monitoring European Integration* (ch. 1, n. 1), Table 2.2.

23 UNECE, *Economic Survey of Europe* (n. 14, above), Table 2.2.13.

24 Ibid., Table 2.2.11.

25 Ibid.; and *The Financial Times*, 9 April 1991.

26 *The Financial Times*, 6 February and 26 March 1991.

27 *The Economist*, 30 January and 23 February 1991; *The Financial Times*, 16 April 1991.

28 *The Financial Times*, 10 April 1991.

29 *The Economist*, 23 February 1991.

30 UNECE, *Economic Survey of Europe* (n. 14, above), Table 2.2.6.

31 *The Financial Times*, 9 April 1991; *The Independent*, 22 February 1991.

32 *The Financial Times*, 18 January 1990.

33 *The Financial Times*, 11 June 1990, 1 November 1990, 22 November 1990, 24 January 1991, and Survey, 4 February 1991; UNECE, *Economic Survey of Europe* (n. 14, above), Tables 2.2.3, 2.2.6, B8.

34 For Soviet economic problems and reforms, see Anders Åslund, *Gorbachev's Struggle for Economic Reform*, London, Pinter, 1989; Commission of the EC, 'Stabilization, Liberalization and Devaluation' (n. 14, above); IMF et al., *The Economy of the USSR* (n. 14, above); UNECE, *Economic Survey of Europe* (n. 14, above).

35 'The Soviet Union' (n. 12, above), p. 15.

36 *The Financial Times*, 11 March and 10 April 1991.

37 *The Financial Times*, 15 April 1991.

Chapter 5

1 Commission of the EC, *Association agreements with the countries of Central and Eastern Europe: a general outline*, Communication from the Commission to the Council and Parliament, COM/90/398 final, Brussels, 27 August 1990. This followed the Commission's *Implications of recent changes in central and eastern Europe for the Community's relations with*

the countries concerned, Communication from the Commission to the
Council, SEC(90)111 final, 23 January 1990; *The development of the
Community's relations with the countries of Central and Eastern Europe*,
SEC(90)196 final, 1 February 1990; *The development of the Community's
relations with the countries of Central and Eastern Europe*, SEC(90)717
final, 18 April 1990.

2 Negotiating Directives for Association Agreements with Poland, Czechoslovakia, Hungary, 11043/90, 11044/90, 11045/90, Brussels, Council of the
EC, 19 December 1990.

3 *Agence Europe*, 29 December 1990.

4 *Agence Europe*, 20 December 1990.

5 Commission of the EC, *Association agreements* (n. 1, above).

6 Adrian Hewitt, *Reform of Tariff Preferences Revisited*, paper for seminar
on 'The Future of the European Community's Generalized System of
Preferences', Brussels, European Institute for South and South–East Asian
Studies, 8 November 1990, p. 6.

7 *Memorandum* presented by Hungary to the EC, Budapest, 12 July 1990.

8 See Friedl Weiss, 'The Legal Issues', and Helen Wallace and Wolfgang
Wessels, 'Conclusions', in Helen Wallace (ed.), *The Wider Western
Europe: Reshaping the EC/EFTA Relationship*, London, RIIA/Pinter, 1991.

9 CEPR, *Monitoring European Integration* (ch. 1, n. 1), pp. 14–19; Gros and
Steinherr, 'Problems, Differences and Similarities' (ch. 4, n. 18), pp. 49–
52.

10 Péter Balázs, 'New Opportunities for Integration in Central–Eastern
Europe', *The International Spectator*, Rome, July–September 1990, p. 187.

11 Arguments for convertibility at a stable exchange rate are reviewed in
Portes, *The Transition to Convertibility* (ch. 4, n. 16); and in Michael
Davenport, *Pegging to the ECU: An Exchange Rate Strategy for Eastern
Europe*, AMEX Bank Review Award Essay, London, American Express,
1990.

12 See for example Portes, *The Transition to Convertibility* (ch. 4, n. 16); P.
Bofinger, *A multilateral payments union for Eastern Europe?*, CEPR
Discussion Paper no. 458, London, CEPR, 1990; UNECE, *Economic
Survey of Europe 1989–90*, New York, United Nations, 1990; *Transitional
Arrangements for Trade and Payments among the CMEA countries*, WP/
90/79, Washington, IMF, 1990.

13 *The Financial Times*, 27 November 1990; *The Economist*, 1 December
1990.

14 Béla Kádár, 'The 1992 Challenge: Responses in East–West Cooperation
and in Hungary', *International Spectator*, Rome, July–September 1990,
p. 170.

15 *Agence Europe*, 11/12 February 1991.

16 Kádár, 'The 1992 Challenge' (n. 14, above), p. 170.

17 This point is stressed in von Staden, 'Das vereinigte Deutschland in Europa' (ch. 1, n. 7), p. 689.
18 *The Financial Times* editorial, 7 January 1991.

Chapter 6

1 Commission of the EC, *Association agreements* (ch. 3, n. 16); and *Declaration of the EEC–Yugoslav Cooperation Council on the Future of Relations between the Community and Yugoslavia*, CEE–YU 1005/90, Brussels, Commission of the EC, 18 December 1990.
2 For confederal alternatives, see Paul Landvai, 'Jugoslawien ohne Jugoslawen: Die Wurzeln der Staatskrise', *Europa-Archiv* 19/1990.
3 *Agence Europe*, 16 February 1991.
4 Commission of the EC, *Association agreements* (ch. 3, no. 16).
5 *The Financial Times*, 12 July 1990.
6 IMF et al., *The Economy of the USSR*, and Commission of the EC, *European Economy no. 45* (ch. 4, n. 14).
7 *Conclusions of the European Council, Rome 14/15 December 1990*, Commission of the EC, Brussels, December 1990.
8 E. P. Wellenstein, 'Een Energiegemeenschap met de Sovjetunie', *Nieuw Europa*, December 1990, p. 178.
9 Commission of the EC, 'Outline proposal for a European Energy Charter', *Agence Europe*, Europe Documents, 15 February 1991.
10 *The Financial Times*, Supplement, 12 March 1990, p. 18.
11 *The Financial Times*, 14 February 1991.
12 CEPR, *Monitoring European Integration* (ch. 1, n. 1), pp. 14–19; Gros and Steinherr, 'Problems, Differences and Similarities' (ch. 4, n. 18), pp. 49–52.
13 *The Financial Times*, 26 February 1991.

Chapter 7

1 CEPR, *Monitoring European Integration* (ch. 1, n. 1), pp. 38–9.
2 Bank for International Settlements, 'Recent Developments in the External Payments and Financing of Central and Eastern European Countries', *International Banking and Financial Market Developments*, Basle, BIS, February 1991.
3 *The Financial Times*, 15 April 1991.
4 These and the statistics in the following text are based on the Commission's *PHARE Scoreboard* (ch. 3, n. 11).
5 See Directorate General for External Relations, *Operation PHARE*, 1/646/90 EN, Commission of the EC, Brussels, 29 November 1990; *Indicative Programme for European Community Assistance to Hungary (PHARE)*, 14

December 1990; *Indicative Programme for European Community Assistance to Poland*, 18 December 1990.

6 *The Financial Times*, 18 January 1990.

7 For this and other lessons from Third World experience, see Christopher Stevens (ed.), *Reform in Eastern Europe: The Third World Dimension*, Overseas Development Institute, London, forthcoming 1991.

8 *Agence Europe*, 11/12 February 1991.

9 See Michael Shackleton, *Financing the European Community*, RIIA/Pinter, London, 1990, Chapter 2.

10 President Delors, address to the European Parliament, 23 January 1991.

11 UN Economic Commission for Europe, *Economic Bulletin for Europe*, vol. 42/90, New York, United Nations, 1990, p. 38.

12 Ibid.; and World Bank estimate, cit. in *The Financial Times*, 7 September 1990.

13 Communication from Vice-President Christopherson in Agreement with Vice-President Andriessen, *An Economic Overview of the Reform Process in the Countries of Central and Eastern Europe*, Brussels, Commission of the EC, 23 April 1990.

14 CEPR, *Monitoring European Integration* (ch. 1, n. 1), p. 38.

15 *Agence Europe*, 10–11 December 1990.

16 Commission of the EC, *Action Plan* (ch. 3, n. 10).

17 See CEPR, *Monitoring European Integration* (ch. 1, n. 1), Table 2.2, p. 33.

18 *The Independent*, 29 November 1990.

19 *PHARE Scoreboard*, (ch. 3, n. 11).

20 For policy implications of Eastern Europe's environmental problems, see Jeremy Russell, *Environmental Issues in Eastern Europe: Setting an Agenda*, London, RIIA and World Conservation Union, 1990.

21 *Bonner Rundschau*, 16 November 1990; *The Financial Times*, 18 April 1991.

22 Gordon Hughes, *Are the Costs of Cleaning up Eastern Europe Exaggerated? Economic Reform and the Environment*, Discussion Paper no. 482, London, CEPR, November 1990.

23 CEPR, *Monitoring European Integration* (ch. 1, n. 1), pp. 38–9.

24 *The Independent*, 4 December 1990.

25 President Delors, address to the European Parliament, 17 January 1990.

26 For an evaluation of its relevance, see Alan Kirman and Lucrezia Reichlin, 'L'aide aux pays de l'Est: les leçons du plan Marshall', in Jean-Paul Fitoussi (ed.), *A l'Est, en Europe: Des économies en transition*, Paris, Presses de la Fondation Nationale des Sciences Politiques, 1990.

27 See Richard Portes, *The European Community and Eastern Europe after 1992*, Occasional Paper no. 3, London, CEPR, October 1990, p. 15.

28 *The Financial Times*, 15 February 1991.

29 H. S. Reuss and Henry P. Smith III, 'Complete the Marshall Plan',

Christian Science Monitor, 23 February 1990.

30 Edward Mortimer, 'Where are you, Marshall and Monnet?', *The Financial Times*, 10 July 1990.

31 *The Financial Times*, 28 December 1989.

32 Delors address (n. 25, above); and *The Financial Times*, 20 March 1990.

33 *Conclusions of the European Council, Rome 14/15 December 1990*, Brussels, Commission of the EC, December 1990.

34 IMF et al., *The Economy of the USSR*, and Commission of the EC, *European Economy no. 45* (ch. 4, n. 14).

35 *The Financial Times*, 11 July 1990 (editorial); 19 May 1991; 22 May 1991.

36 *The Financial Times*, Supplement, 12 March 1990, p. 19; see also n. 21, above.

Chapter 8

1 Von Staden, 'Das vereinigte Deutschland in Europa' (ch. 1, n. 7), p. 688.

2 Kohl, 'Die Rolle Deutschlands' (ch. 1, n. 5).

3 See for example, 'De europese politieke unie' (ch. 1, n. 11), pp. 23–4.

4 John Pinder, *European Community: The Building of a Union*, Oxford and New York, Oxford University Press, 1991.